LEICESTERSHIRE
& RUTLAND
FOLK
TALES

LEICESTERSHIRE & RUTLAND

FOLK TALES

LEICESTERSHIRE GUILD
OF STORYTELLING

The
History
Press

First published 2013
Reprinted 2017

The History Press
The Mill, Brimscombe Port
Stroud, Gloucestershire, GL5 2QG
www.thehistorypress.co.uk

British Library Cataloguing in Publication Data.
A catalogue record for this book is available from the British Library.

ISBN 978 0 7524 8578 2

Typesetting and origination by The History Press
Printed in Great Britain by TJ Books Ltd, Padstow, Cornwall.

CONTENTS

Rutland, the country's smallest county, has, throughout history, been closely connected with Leicestershire. As recently as 1974 until 1997, Rutland was part of Leicestershire. However, after a well-fought campaign it is now a proudly independent county. It seemed appropriate, therefore, to include tales from Rutland with those from Leicestershire.

INTRODUCTION

Some twenty years ago, having already spent a few years telling stories in schools, I realised that there was an upsurge of many different storytelling events – storytelling for everyone that is, not just for youngsters – happening in Leicester. We had already established a regular pub meeting, 'Lies and Legends', at the Rainbow & Dove; NATE storytellers at the School of Education were active; Earthtales, the first environmental storytelling events, were about to take place; and Leicester's fledgling Comedy Festival had included some storytelling evenings in their programme. But, above all, the Phoenix Arts Centre had booked the Company of Storytellers – Ben Haggarty, Sally Pomme Clayton and Hugh Lupton – to present 'The Three Snake Leaves', after which Ben would be leading two workshops. From the December of 1994 and the end of February 1995 there would be nineteen storytelling performances, workshops or discussions around the theme of the told story in Leicester.

At about this time I happened to be showing a friend the sights in Leicester. I took her into the Guildhall and found that there was a fire set in the great fireplace, all ready for an evening meeting. Looking around at the space, and imagining the fire lit, I knew that this would be the most wonderful place in which to hear stories told. Leicester already had stories in pubs – informal, and with lots of room for contributions from the floor – tales could be heard in woods and outdoors (Earthtales), and children and teachers were well catered for by NATE. There was one thing missing – a regular series of performance storytelling events: a programme of storytellers from around the world, telling the traditional tales of the past and the great myths of the beginnings of time. There could be no better place to host such a programme than the Guildhall.

We owe much to Nick Ladlaw, the Guildhall manager at that time, and to all the staff, for, without exception, they were highly enthusiastic and unbelievably helpful in their response to my suggestion that we might present an evening of stories in front of the fire in the Great Hall. So it was that in the winter of 1995 I carried a four-branched lighted candleholder down the stairs leading from the Old Town Library, into the packed Great Hall, to tell a selection of stories entitled 'Magical Women': the first event in the programme of storytelling at the Guildhall.

With so much happening in the city and around, it seemed important to bring together the information concerning these different events, so I put together an initial leaflet (very amateur) and with Nick's help, and encouragement from Oliver Savage of Environ and Judy Hughes of the Phoenix Theatre, organised a meeting at which the Guild of Storytelling was formed. Our aim, as stated on the first professionally produced leaflet, is 'to promote storytelling both as an art form and in its educational uses through coordination of publicity and joint promotion of events'. And storytelling in Leicester was set to flourish.

In the nature of things, some events came to an end; but for the next twelve years a programme of performance storytelling at the Guildhall became a well-attended and much appreciated feature of the arts scene in the city. We have heard performers from India, New Zealand, France and the USA. We have also heard Aboriginal tellers, Gipsy tellers and many others. And, of course, storytellers from the four corners of the British Isles, telling traditional tales, comic stories, ancient Greek myths, stories with music and stories with food. To all we owe a heartfelt thanks, but special thanks must go to the Company of Storytellers – Ben, Pomme and Hugh – who have entertained and delighted us so many times over the years and have taught both audiences and other storytellers just how powerful the told story can be.

The Guild of Storytelling itself has grown smaller over time and has concentrated on the programme at the Guildhall. A small group of us have devised programmes, filled in funding applications, organised publicity and raised funds to support the programme by group performances. So it seemed right that when we were approached to put together folk tales of

Leicestershire and Rutland that this too should be a group effort. In reading these stories you will hear five different voices; these voices belong to Kath Chalk, Mike Chalk, Jill Jobson, Terry Jobson and Liza Watts. We hope that you enjoy them.

Thanks must also go to the many storytellers who have travelled to the Guildhall in Leicester, and to the people who, over the years, have been part of the Guild, but have since moved away or moved on to better things.

Liza Watts

1

GOSSIP

Close by the cathedral church of St Martin stands an ancient building with steeply pitched roofs – Leicester's Guildhall, one of the best-preserved timber-framed halls in the country. An historic building of importance nationally, it is still in constant use.

The oldest part of the building, the eastern bay of the Great Hall, dates back to around 1390 and was built by the newly formed Guild of Corpus Christi. The Guild was a lay religious body of men who worshipped together in their chapel in the church of St Martin's, supported each other in times of bereavement or need, and feasted together in celebration of religious festival days. An important group of men, the Guild of Corpus Christi was to become a powerful force in the life of medieval Leicester. Extended over the centuries, Corpus Christi Hall remained the meeting place of the Guild until the Dissolution of the Monasteries in the reign of King Henry VIII. The building then became the town hall and remained the centre of the town's governance until a new town hall was built on Horse Fair in 1876. The old town hall is known today simply as the Guildhall.

Standing in the Great Hall, with the cold of the flagstoned floor underfoot and the dark timbers of the roof trusses above, the noise of our twenty-first-century city is muffled. The stairs leading from the hall to the Old Town Library creak, though no one treads them, and there is a powerful sense of long-gone times.

There are two fireplaces in the hall; the later one has a stone overmantel and is still used on occasion. The building originally had an earth floor, probably rush-strewn, and was heated by an open hearth in the centre of the hall. Smoke from this fire would have drifted upwards, finding its way out through the roof. Lift the removable flagstone, and a glass covering now sits atop the pit of this ancient hearth. The jawbone of a boar can be seen in the hearth – the discarded remains of a feast, bones thrown aside by our medieval forebears as they gathered about their fire, coughing, spitting, chewing at pieces of meat, and gossiping.

Gossip. The lifeblood of the told story. And the subject of that gossip? All too often the Church, the priest, or the monks of the abbey, and the curious stories and strange beliefs which cling to the lives of the devout, the saintly.

THE MONK OF LEICESTER

There was once, in old Leicester, a monk of the abbey that lay in that town. Of middling years, he was of more than middling height and of goodly weight and bore before him a fine round belly. His face it too was round, with coloured cheeks. His hands they were small, white and plump with well-trimmed nails, for he was a scribe and spent long hours with quill and colour, labouring at the manuscripts of the abbey.

Now, as he sat penning his fffs and his ttts, he would pause and gaze at his plump white hand, and then the Devil tempted him with visions; visions of that hand laid not upon the parchment, but rather upon a soft white thigh, a full round breast. For our monk, by name Dan Hugh, was a lusty and lascivious monk, much given to ogling the young maidens and to waylaying the wives and widows of the town.

He had, at the time of my tale, caught glimpses of a certain young woman newly arrived in Leicester. Small and slender, with a delicate upturned nose and eyes that seemed to laugh at the world around her, she was the bride of a wealthy and somewhat elderly tailor of the town. Dan Hugh was much taken with her; there was none so fair, so exciting, in all of Leicester. He was determined; he would have some dalliance with the plump and comely young woman. He would accost the tailor's wife, come what may.

As he went about the town he watched for her, and one day found her in the marketplace, buying fish for her husband's table. He stood close, too close, peered down at her, breathed into her face and began to sing:

> A monk there was in Leicester as I've heard many tell
> He saw a handsome witty wife, and loved her full well.

Knowing the song, and not liking to hear it so misquoted, she blushed and tried to push past him. He blocked her way.

'Come my beauty, walk with me.'

'Hush sir, let me pass. Let me be, I beg you.'

Walking as fast as she could – he still at her heels, urging his suit and proclaiming his love so loud that all around could hear – she tried to escape him. Embarrassed and harassed, angry yet tearful, she turned to face him just as Dan Hugh managed to reach out and clasp her round the waist. As he did so he whispered, 'See the purse at my belt? It has gold coins, two golden pieces. One for you my love, when you grant me my desire.'

Now, though newly-wed and loving her husband just as any good wife should, the young woman had realised very soon after her wedding that her bridegroom was overly careful with his wealth. The gold coin in the purse at the monk's belt would be most useful. She paused and looked at the monk, 'Come tomorrow, at noon, when my husband will be from home.'

Happy, Dan Hugh released his hold of her, stepped back and bowed. She walked swiftly home.

At home the tailor questioned her, 'Come wife, what news from the market?'

'Why husband, news of a most importunate, lusty monk.'

'What of that monk, wife?'

'He comes here tomorrow to make love to your wife.'

'Indeed. And you, wife, would play me false would you?'

'No sir, that I would not. And therefore I beg that you be at home before noon tomorrow, and let me hide you in the closet before sir monk is come.'

'And what then my witty wife?'

'You shall be witness to my honesty, and spring out to save me.'

The next day Dan Hugh made his way to the house of the tailor, and, taking the woman in his arms, dangled the purse before her eyes.

'Now my beauty, let us make fine sport together.'

'Indeed sir, but first allow me to put your purse away, lest in our enjoyment and delight the golden coins from your purse should roll to the floor and be lost between the boards.'

Taking the purse with its two golden coins, she went to the closet and opened it. Then out sprang the tailor with a cudgel in his hand and straightaway began to beat the monk about the head. Two blows, three blows, four, and the monk staggered, swayed and fell to the floor.

Dead. Quite dead. Thus was Dan Hugh first slain.

'Alas husband, is he dead?' cried the wife. 'What's to be done with him? We shall surely be hanged if he be discovered here. Husband, let me think. Hush now, never fear. I have it. When it has grown dark, you must take this false priest to the abbey. Soon he will begin to stiffen. Stand him against the wall by the gate to the abbey.'

So, in the darkness, the tailor did as his wife had instructed him and carried the body of the monk back to the abbey and left him leaning nonchalantly against the old stone wall.

Near midnight the abbot, calling for Dan Hugh and not finding him anywhere within the abbey, bade a young novice to accompany him and set out to find Hugh. As the two went out the gate, they saw the figure of the monk propped up against the wall.

'Rogue, art thou drunk? Why dost thou neglect the holy service? Come speak. What no explanation? No word? Then I'll box your ears to open your mouth,' and the abbot clenched his fists and pummelled him about the head till once more Dan Hugh fell to the ground.

Dead. Well and truly dead. Thus was he slain a second time.

'Sir Abbot! You have killed Dan Hugh.'

'Aye, he's dead indeed. But he must most certainly not be found here. A gold piece for you to take him and put him elsewhere. Aye, let the good monk be found anywhere but here by the abbey.'

Now, the novice had watched Dan Hugh follow the tailor's wife, and understood the monk's lecherous intentions. He knew, also, that the tailor was an extremely jealous husband, quite capable of wounding, or even killing, any man he suspected of having designs on his young wife. So the novice took the body back to the tailor's house and left it just outside the door. In his sleep the tailor stirred, heard a scuffling at his door, woke, climbed out of bed and peered from the window. In the darkness he did not see the novice creep away, but could just make out the shape of a body at his door.

'Wife, wife, the monk! The monk – he has come back to trouble us! Alas, alas wife. Now what's to be done? For sure the dead can walk.'

'Let me think, husband. Hush, hush now. What's to be done with this importunate dead monk? I have it. You shall put the wretch in a sack and cast him into the river. Hurry, before it grows light.'

So the tailor took the sack, stuffed with the goodly weight of the monk's body, through the dark streets of Leicester. He was nearing the mill which stood at a bend in the river, and he could hear the rush of the mill race, when he saw the door to the miller's house open. Fearing to be seen with his burden, the tailor dropped the sack and fled, running as fast as he could for home. However, it was not the burly miller who emerged from the mill; it was a thief. And the thief, Sammy by name, was also carrying a sack. In this sack was a fine side of bacon stolen from the miller's kitchen, for Sammy's wife was particularly partial to a slice or two of fat bacon to eat with her tea.

Sammy was creeping away with the bacon when the dogs began to bark. A window was flung open and the miller thrust his head out and roared, 'Thief! Stop thief, stop. Stop villain.' Terrified, Sammy threw away his burden and hid himself under a bush. The miller came out from his house, carrying a lighted candle, and began to search for the thief. But then the wind got up, and quite suddenly the candle was blown out. The miller retired back to his bed, cursing the dark night, the wind, and all thieving rascals.

When all was quiet, out from his hiding place crept Sammy, and he felt around in the darkness for the sack. Finding it at last he hurried off home to wake his wife and to feast upon fat bacon. 'A feast, in the middle of the night, my dear.'

She was so hungry for bacon that she could barely wait to draw water and put on the kettle. After opening the sack with a knife, she plunged her hand in. No bacon there; instead – oh horror, horror – a dead monk.

'Merciful heavens – you have killed Dan Hugh and we shall both be hanged if it be discovered.'

'But wife, I had this sack from the miller's kitchen. It was not I that killed the good monk; it must be the miller that did this deed. I shall return it to him now, while it is still night. It must hang again on the hook in his kitchen.'

So was Dan Hugh twice slain and once hung.

Early the next day the miller's wife went to cut her husband a slice of the bacon but found, in its stead, the body of the monk. Calling the miller, they considered what to do, and agreed it was best to send him back to the abbey.

They put an old helmet on the dead man's head, found a shield to strap about his chest, and put a sword in his hand. Then they bound him so that he sat, straight as any warrior knight, upon the back of their best donkey. Next the miller led the animal to the gate of the abbey and waited. When the gate opened he whipped the donkey so that she brayed loudly and galloped into the courtyard of the abbey. At the same time the miller blew on his horn and cried out, 'Wake, wake my masters! An enemy is come to put all to the sword, arm yourselves.'

The monks were thrown into confusion, gathered what weapons they could find and ran out to do battle. They thrust swords at the figure on the donkey, hurled stones and shot arrows at the rider, till Dan Hugh crashed to the ground.

Dead. Absolutely dead. Thus was the monk of Leicester once hung and three times slain.

And so our story ends, for this time his fellow monks they buried him. They buried that lusty monk with prayers, with 'bell, book and candle', so that, as far as we know, he remained thereafter well and truly dead and buried.

THE TAILOR OF LEICESTER

And here is yet another story of our lusty monk of Leicester. Was there such a man, one wonders?

A tailor lived in Leicester as I've heard many tell
He had a handsome witty wife who loved him full well
But he was touched with jealousy, as often you may hear
Which made that handsome witty wife for to shed many a tear.

And after she had wiped the tear from her eye, that handsome, witty wife sat herself down by the fire and considered by what means she could cure her husband of his excessive jealousy. The fire crackled and she could hear the soup, which was simmering in the pot above the flames, begin to bubble and boil. She took a spoon and stirred. Potatoes, onions, a good handful of thyme from the garden, and the fine fat carp that she had bought from the market early that very morning. She stirred slowly, carefully, and as she stirred a plan began to form in her head.

It was soon time to remove the bones from the bubbling soup. The flesh slipped easily, gently, from the bones as she pulled the fishy skeleton from out the pot. Now she knew what she must do; the next time the monk Don Hugh, who plagued her so with his unwanted attentions, approached her, she would seem to listen kindly to his protestations of love, would seem to welcome these attentions. She would invite him to visit her, to dine with her one evening when her husband was supposedly away from home. In the meantime she must warn the tailor, and persuade him to secrete himself in the closet on the fateful evening and leap out to save her from the lusty monk.

Her honesty in the face of an admirer's advances would surely restore the tailor's faith in her honour.

So, one evening, the monk made his way to the house of the tailor. The tailor was well hidden in the closet. Once again the wife had cooked a dish of boiled carp and she and the monk were seated at the table. In the closet the tailor could hear snatches of their talk, then the clink of spoons and the slurp of soup being supped. The rich smell of onions and carp seeped into the closet, tickling the tailor's nose, tempting his taste buds. He could bear it no longer. Was it his greed, or was it the need to save the honour of his handsome wife, that drove the tailor to burst from his hiding place brandishing a very large cudgel and lunge at the monk?

Startled, Don Hugh gulped down an enormous, succulent mouthful of carp soup, coughed, spluttered and struggled for breath. A fish bone had clamped itself firmly inside his throat. A very large and persistent bone; a stubborn and determined bone. The monk gasped, struggled, turned bright red, then white and then blue and fell to the floor. He lay twisting, squirming on the floor until, at last, his body ceased its writhing and the lusty monk was dead.

The tailor looked at his wife. 'Oh wife, what have we done? Most surely he is dead, and we shall both be hanged.'

'Courage, my dear, take courage, for none know that he was to come here. Let us carry him back to the abbey, so it may appear he died of eating fish from the monks' table.'

The tailor put the body on a small cart and wheeled it through the dark streets of Leicester to the abbey. There he leaned Don Hugh against the old stone wall and crept back home, where he settled down to what was left of the dish of boiled carp.

Later that night the abbot's serving man was returning to the abbey after a very happy evening in the alehouse, when he spotted the body leaning against the wall. He greeted the figure, but got no answer. This silence on the part of the monk enraged the servant and, being as they say 'in his cups', he set about beating the body till it slumped to the ground. Don Hugh did not stir. The serving man kicked at the body. Still no response, no movement. He peered into the monk's face and realised that this was a very dead monk. 'Alas, alas, he's dead, so help me Lord. Dead by my hand and I shall surely hang for it. Dead, dead. Alas and woe to me.'

Now the serving man remembered what manner of monk Don Hugh had been. A lusty and greedy monk, much given to all carnal delights, to the pleasures of the flesh and of drink and food, especially to the enjoyment of sweet things, cakes and sweetmeats. And so he thought it would be good to put the body near to the baker's shop.

In the darkness, the serving man stumbled over a stone, dropped the body and then blindly endeavoured to stand the dead man next to the door of the bakery. Hearing the noise, the baker woke from sleep, climbed from his warm bed and peered out of his window. In the dim light, the baker saw a figure apparently intent upon entering his shop. Immediately, he seized the chamber pot and hurled it at the intruder. The baker's aim was good; he hit his target and the apparent thief toppled to the ground and lay there, unmoving.

Very pleased with himself, the baker hurried downstairs to apprehend the thief, but was much dismayed to find him dead. 'I never intended to kill the fellow. Most surely I will hang for this. Must move the body. Let me think. Here's the river close by, there be sacks in the mill. He shall go into a sack and thence into the river.'

And Don Hugh was cast into the water; first he sank to the bottom, then he rose and, escorted by shoals of fish, slowly, lazily, he drifted downstream. There the constable fished him from the water, and saw that the sack was marked Finest White Flour. Who but a baker would have sacks marked Finest White Flour? The baker was promptly arrested, taken before the justice and sentenced to hang.

The gallows stood ready, the justice waited, and an eager crowd was gathering. The constable led out the convicted man, the hangman stood ready with the noose, the priest prayed the last prayer and the baker prepared to meet his maker. The noose was put round his neck and the crowd grew silent when, in the silence, up spoke the abbot's serving man. 'Stop! Don't hang the baker, hang me. 'Twas I that cudgelled the monk to death, for he would not speak and angered me with his silence. Don't hang the baker. Hang me.'

And now the justice pronounced the baker innocent, and on the guilty serving man he passed sentence of death by hanging. The priest prayed the last prayer, the hangman took the noose from round the neck of the baker and placed it round the neck of the serving man, and the serving man made ready to meet his maker. The jeering and the laughter of the crowd stilled. They waited. And in the silence, up spoke the tailor. 'Stop! Don't hang the serving man, for it was at my house the monk died. Don't hang the serving man. Hang me.'

And the judge was adjusting his black cap, was preparing to pronounce sentence upon the tailor, when 'Stop!' cried the tailor's wife. 'Don't hang the serving man, don't hang the baker, and don't hang my husband. Hang me, for I cooked the carp that harboured the bone that lodged in the throat that choked the monk.'

Now the justice looked at the constable, the constable looked at the hangman, the hangman looked the crowd and the crowd just looked at the gallows, till in the silence a small voice could be heard. 'Stop! Don't hang the tailor, don't hang the tailor's wife. Don't hang the baker, don't hang the serving man. Hang the fish, hang the carp, hang the fish bone.'

And they did just that. After, that is, the whole sorry saga had been reported to the King, who demanded to hear the story not once, not twice, but three times, and laughed and laughed and laughed. And when the King had wiped the tears of laughter from his eyes, he declared that henceforth, every year, upon the anniversary of the day, he would dine only upon the finest dish in the land – a dish of onions with boiled carp.

NICODEMUS

In the late nineteenth century, George Sanders and his sister Selina lived in the village of Cossington in a house near the village pound. George had some very strange habits. He would wrap his head in a towel and parade around the streets in a long, light-coloured coat that swept the ground as he walked. He had deep staring eyes and long, dark, straggly hair. His appearance and behaviour frightened the local children and disconcerted many of the adults. He was so odd that the villagers called him Nicodemus; a strange name to fit a strange man.

Though Nicodemus was never known to go out to work, he seemed to live as well as anyone else in the village. On Sunday he went twice to the parish church. There he was given money from the poor box. On Monday he was to be seen at Mass at Ratcliffe College, professing himself a Catholic. On Wednesday he was a Primitive Methodist, worshipping in a nearby village. And by Friday he had become a Baptist, attending meetings at

any distant village to which the carrier's cart could convey him. He did very well, as they say!

But when the vicar, Revd Chetto, got to hear of Nicodemus's ecumenical rounds, he became much less generous with his handouts. As the rector's beneficence dried up, people in the village began to notice that produce was disappearing overnight from their gardens. Some of the villagers swore that they saw a pale shape wandering through the village in the dead of night, and were convinced that a ghost had come to reside among them. They had seen it drifting about, wrapped in its winding sheet. Soon it was agreed by all that there really was a ghost stealing their produce. And that it could be dangerous to be abroad in darkness.

Now Revd Chetto was much better educated than his parishioners and was not prone to superstitions. It occurred to him that ghosts do not generally have a need for cabbages and carrots as grown in local gardens. He let it be known that he had a really good crop of plums in his garden that year and he would be picking them on the following Monday. (It was obviously not something that a pious man of the cloth could do on a Sunday.)

On Saturday night Revd Chetto, accompanied by his fierce mastiff, Griffin, hid behind a bush in the rectory garden and waited patiently. As all the lights in the village went out and everyone went to bed, it became very dark. Not a sound could be heard except for the rustling of small animals in the undergrowth. Then, sure enough, at about 1 a.m., the rector saw a pale shape flitting among his trees. It was busy filling a sack with his ripe plums. With a shout, the rector released Griffin and set him at the intruder. The ghost turned tail, running like the wind. It had two legs and was definitely not floating through the air. In a mighty bound it leapt over the fence, but not before Griffin had managed to get a mouthful of 'winding sheet' and leg. With a blood-curdling shriek the apparition disappeared into the night.

The following Sunday, Revd Chetto noted that Nicodemus's light-coloured coat was decidedly more ragged than previously. He also saw that Nicodemus now walked with a very noticeable limp. As for the 'ghost', well, it was never seen again!

BEEBY TUB

All too often gossip turns out to have an element of truth in its roots. This sad little tale of two brothers would seem to have a basis in fact.

When visitors to the small village of Beeby first see the church, they often ask what happened to the spire. Did it fall down? The reason for their question is that on the top of the tower is just a small stub of a spire, hence its name, Beeby Tub.

The story is that two masons, the brothers Denys and Hugh, were engaged by the abbot of Leicester to construct a church in the nearby village of Queniborough. The abbot was delighted with the plans. The church was built with a magnificent spire that could be seen for miles around.

Sometime later, the abbot of Croyland, who owned the manor of Beeby, went to see how the building of his new church there was progressing. Looking over the fields towards the next village of Queniborough, he could see in the distance the church with its magnificent spire. He was so impressed with the sight that he thought he must have a similar spire on his church, for nothing could be too good for the House of God.

The abbot wrote to the abbot of Leicester enquiring which masons had been responsible for erecting the spire on the church at Queniborough. The answer came back, and Denys and Hugh were engaged to build a spire on the tower of the church at Beeby. A spire which would rise up towards the heavens, to the glory of God.

The brothers undertook the work, but from the start there was trouble. They could not agree on the plans. Hugh said that the tower would not be strong enough to support the spire as drawn up by his brother Denys.

'And,' he said, 'likely the money'll run out before the spire's ever built.'

Denys argued that the money would be provided by the abbot, and said, 'Anyways, money's not our concern, spire is.'

So, without any agreement between the brothers, the tower was completed and the workers began on the spire. Eventually it had risen to just above the battlements of the tower, and promised to look just as magnificent as the spire on the church at Queniborough. Then came the fateful day. The brothers were standing together up on the tower by the base of the spire. They were arguing yet again about whether the tower would take the full weight of the tall spire. Denys seemed determined to see it built at all costs.

'The money has run out,' argued Hugh, 'The workers won't work for nothing. They need paying; they need paying now.'

Denys, increasingly exasperated by his brother's common-sense concerns, turned on Hugh and pushed him, punching him hard. Hugh stumbled, clutching at Denys to save himself. Unfortunately he caught Denys off balance, and, clinging together, the two brothers toppled off the tower, falling on the stack of stones below. Stones that were waiting to be hauled up to build the spire.

Following the death of the two brothers, it was decided not to complete the spire. Instead it was given a roof, a mere stump in place of the planned magnificent spire. It remains so to this day and is known far and wide as Beeby Tub.

> Beeby Tub was to have been a spire;
> Two brothers fought, and broke their necks; and so 'twas built no higher.

(*Nichols' History of Leicestershire*, 1800)

St Wistan

It happened hundreds of years ago in the middle of the ninth century, in the Kingdom of Mercia, which stretched across the middle of what is now England.

Brifardus was deeply disappointed, and indeed very angry. How could they make weedy little Wistan the heir to the Kingdom of Mercia? He, Brifardus, was the son of the King of Mercia, King Bertwulf, so he should be the heir! Well alright, he knew that his uncle Wiglaf had been king before his father, and that when Wiglaf's son Wigmund died, Wiglaf's grandson Wistan was supposed to succeed. But then Wiglaf had gone and died whilst Wistan was still a little child, far too young to be king, so the West Saxon king had wisely appointed Bertwulf. So he, Brifardus, should be named heir, even if Wistan was older now.

Besides, Wistan wasn't interested in statecraft and ruling. Wistan was only interested in following a religious life. He had even asked his widowed mother Elflaeda to rule as his regent, although he hadn't given up his hereditary rights. This really annoyed Brifardus, for if he didn't want to rule for himself, why on earth didn't he hand over to someone who did want to rule?

Brifardus now began to plot and plan how he might gain what he thought ought to be his rightful position. Plan one: marry Queen Elflaeda, the widow of Wigmund and mother of Wistan. He wrote her a letter which read:

> Let the Queen accept my counsel and be at accord with a man, a man of high nobility, and I will make her my wife, so that my power being united with her rank, she may with more security watch over the rights of the Kingdom.

And did she agree to this? No, indeed she did not! She first consulted her son, and he very emphatically said 'No' and that as Brifardus was his godfather, he could not be his father by marriage as well. 'Also,' he said, 'any marriage between my mother and such a close relative would be incestuous, according to the New Testament.'

So, Wistan's religious scruples having put paid to his schemes, and furious to be so thwarted, Brifardus decided that more drastic measures were called for: Wistan would have to go. With great guile, Brifardus wrote to Wistan, and, with many words of peace and love, invited him to an assembly. This was to be in a part of the kingdom where many earlier national assemblies had taken place, close to Leicester. The actual spot chosen was on land alongside the River Sence. It was there that Brifardus hoped to slay Wistan.

Prince Wistan arrived with a grand retinue, as was customary for a prince in that time. Unfortunately for him, and foolishly as it turned out, none of his company was armed. Brifardus, of course, had come with an equally grand company, but he had ensured that all his men were armed, their weapons being well hidden beneath their cloaks. Wistan was invited to walk apart from his men and to give and receive the kiss of peace. Suspecting nothing, Wistan agreed. In the middle of this solemn rite, Brifardus drew his sword, and, raising it high in the air, brought the hilt crashing down onto the unsuspecting head of Wistan. This was a fatal blow, but to ensure that the Prince was truly dead, one of Brifardus' closest followers thrust his sword into Wistan's back. At least three of Wistan's followers were killed in the ensuing confusion.

So Wistan died, and Brifardus was free to take his place – though he didn't enjoy that triumph for very long.

After his murder, Wistan's body was taken from the place where he was slain to the nearby village of Wigston, to prepare for the onward journey to his final resting place at Repton in what is now Derbyshire. Repton was the capital of Mercia, and it was there, in the monastic church, that many of its kings and princes were buried.

In the days and weeks after his burial, reports of miracles grew. From the very spot where Wistan had fallen, there rose a

column of light which ascended towards heaven. It was said to have been visible from all around the country, and to shine for thirty days. After thirty days the light disappeared, thus proving to the devout that God had witnessed the death of one of his martyrs.

His martyrdom was further confirmed on the anniversary of his death, when on the very spot where his shattered skull had fallen to the ground, a miraculous growth of human hair was seen to sprout from the earth. This happened every 1 June, on the very day and at the exact time of his martyrdom. For one amazing hour, these human hairs were to be seen growing amongst the grasses. And thereafter was he called St Wistan.

All these miracles and stories were enough to drive a person crazy. And they did. Brifardus went mad, lost his position and everyone agreed that it was God's judgement working upon him.

In time a church dedicated to St Wistan was built close to this site, and the village that grew there was called Wistanstowe (the holy place of St Wistan). It was only in much later years that the name became shortened to Wistow.

At nearby Wigston, where his remains had rested on the journey to Repton, a small shrine was erected, which was later incorporated into a chapel dedicated to St Wistan and supported by an annual pilgrimage made by the people of Wigston.

Many miracles were attributed to St Wistan, though few details have been passed down to us. However, in about 1020 the abbot of Evesham petitioned for the saint's remains to be removed to Evesham, and this was allowed (probably to protect them from invading Danes). Then in 1067 the Norman abbot proved beyond all doubt the sanctity of Wistan's remains;

for, when cast into a fierce fire, they failed to burn. His remains were taken from the flames, examined and pronounced to be totally unscathed.

More than 100 years later, the then Archbishop of Canterbury, on hearing of the miraculous growth of hair at Wistanstowe, wished to have the truth of it checked. He got together a group of religious men, including the abbot of Leicester and the prior of Monks Kirby, and sent them to watch over the sacred site on 1 June. This they did, after fasting and praying for three days beforehand. Great was their joy when, at the appointed hour, they found thick, curly human hair springing up amongst the grasses. These tresses of human hair they both touched and kissed, then noticed and recorded that they disappeared as mysteriously as they had appeared, at the end of the hour. The abbot and his fellow monks then returned to the Archbishop full of praise and thanksgiving for this miraculous event, and in the full hope that many more of the faithful would witness this wondrous happening in the years to follow.

And the exact spot where the miracle is said to have happened? In this day and age, who knows? Now, possibly only with the aid of a few magic mushrooms would anyone be able to observe the 'hair today, gone tomorrow' phenomenon.

THE GRIFFIN OF GRIFFYDAM

Thirteen hundred years ago a monastery was built at Breedon Hill. Today, a very old church still stands there. This church contains many Anglo-Saxon stone carvings and is dedicated to St Mary and St Hardulph. When the monastery was built, the hill was surrounded by thick forests, with assorted clearings for villages and plots of cultivated land.

One morning, about 1,000 years ago, the prior was standing outside the monastery looking out over the forest, which covered the area for as far as the eye could see. Smoke curled up from the villages and small farmsteads, revealing signs of habitation, the homes of people who came to worship on Sundays and holidays. Their donations helped him and his fellow monks to live a very comfortable life in the pleasantest of pleasant surroundings.

His solitary meditation was suddenly interrupted by a small boy. Out of breath, for he had run as fast as he could manage up the steep hill leading to the monastery, the boy fell on his knees begging for help. The prior helped him to stand and asked, 'What is it that troubles you so my son?'

'Oh, Father, there is a very big, nasty, dangerous monster in our well, and no one can get any water for fear of being eaten, and we shall all die of the thirst if it don't go. Please come quickly and make it go away.'

The prior stayed just long enough to collect a small jar of holy water, then set off on the two-mile journey to the village. As they trudged down the stony path, he listened as the boy tried his best to describe the monster.

'Some say it's the Devil!' said the boy, 'Others, they say it's a dragon, for it has these wings, and it has a very big head and mouth with lots of teeth, and a long tail that swishes from side to side.'

At the village the prior peered nervously into the well, studying the strange creature. He noted its eagle-like head and wings, and its body and tail like the body and tail of a lion and, at last, with much shaking of his venerable head,

the prior declared the unwelcome creature to be a griffin. Seeing the beast, he understood full well that his small bottle of holy water would be quite useless. He could do nothing to drive the monster out of the well. They must wait until the creature left of its own free will.

This did not please the villagers, who felt that they had to do something – anything! – to rid themselves of this dreadful creature. So, encouraged by the other men, and watched by a group of excited but fearful children, the butcher stood clutching his two-handed meat cleaver to his chest. He was readying himself to strike the beast. Slowly he lifted the weapon, focused, and hurled it at the monster. The griffin turned its head, opened its great mouth, caught the cleaver and calmly started to munch the wooden handle. It spat out the iron blade with a snarl.

Next the village blacksmith loosed his large hunting dog at the griffin. Growling and biting, the dog jumped into the attack. The griffin turned its head, caught the dog in its beak, and crushed the life out of the poor creature.

All the villagers drew back in fear and horror. They looked at the prior – surely he would have a solution to this problem. However, it was clear to him that there was nothing that could be done; they would just have to wait until such time as the beast went away of its own accord. He feared that they might have a very long wait, a fearful and thirsty wait.

But there was one problem that must be fixed before the griffin decided to depart. The people needed water. The best thing would be to supply them with water to drink from the well near the priory. So, he organised a horse and cart to climb Priory Hill and transport water back by the barrel-load. The village must have water.

Several days later, a passing knight stopped and asked for water for himself and his horse. One villager brought him a small jug. In the jug were just a few inches of water. The villager apologised and explained that they had little enough water, even for their own needs. He went on to tell the knight all about the griffin that had taken over their well and could not be got rid of.

Intrigued, the knight then went to have a look at this strange sight. Having studied the situation thoroughly, he gathered some of the men of the village together, and asked for a strong longbow and three good arrows. The blacksmith hurried to fetch a heavy-weight bow and a selection of arrows from his smithy.

The knight and the griffin eyed each other, the knight moving around trying to get a good position from which to shoot, and the griffin continually turning its head from side to side, watching the knight, following his every move till, confused and angry, the beast opened its beak wide and let out a most fearsome roar. The knight immediately seized his chance, grabbed his arrow, drew his bow back to his eye, sighted down the shaft and loosed the shot. The arrow flew straight down the griffin's throat. It let out a terrible roar and dropped down dead.

By the time the villagers had removed the dead griffin from the well, the knight was long gone and no one knew who he was. It was said that the skin of the griffin was nailed up inside the church, over the door. If it was, it's not there now; but something else is. There is an ancient stone in the church carved with the shape of a griffin.

SIMON DE MONTFORT

The battle raged, steel clashed on armour, horses screamed and men cursed, groaned and bled. The hiss and whine of arrows filled the air and hooves trampled the fallen into the sludge of mud underfoot, while above, the heavens mirrored the struggle taking place on the battlefield of Evesham. The skies turned black as if in outrage at the carnage, lightning forked and thunder growled as, in the August of 1265, Simon de Montfort, Earl of Leicester, fought his last battle. Defeated by King Henry III's forces, his corpse was mutilated by the victorious soldiers, his hands and feet severed, and his testicles cut off and presented to the wife of his bitterest enemy.

At the time of his death on the battlefield, Simon de Montfort was under edict of excommunication and, to make doubly sure, he had received a second dose of papal opprobrium, being excommunicated for a second time by Pope Clement IV's legate. He was certainly not popular with the Vatican.

Handsome, brave, articulate, an attractive man – and, though having a fierce and sudden temper, a charismatic leader – Simon de Montfort had been invested Earl of Leicester in 1239.

He also held the Stewardship of all England, a position which gave him authority to supervise the government of the whole realm. He was married to the King's sister, the Lady Eleanor, but, when in 1264 the disgruntled barons took up arms against King Henry III, Simon sided with them rather than with the King. The brothers-in-law had personal as well as political disagreements to settle.

Under de Montfort's leadership, the rebel barons were victorious in the Battle of Lewes. Henry's army was defeated and the King himself, along with his family, were taken and imprisoned. So, from May 1264 until August 1265, Simon de Montfort ruled England. He formed his first parliament, summoning four knights from each county to take seats at the gathering. To his second parliament a month later, he summoned two burgesses from each town, as well as the four knights from the counties, thus establishing a very early model for the House of Commons.

Unfortunately for de Montfort, the King's eldest son managed to escape his imprisonment, and fighting broke out once more. The young prince, who was later to become Edward I, set free his father the King, and then marched on Evesham to engage with the barons in the battle in which de Montfort would be killed.

So the rebel leader was dead. King Henry's popular and charismatic opponent was no more. Yet somehow the man who had been excommunicated twice by the Vatican became a most unexpected and unlikely candidate for saintly fame. Greatly loved by many people, de Montfort was a particular favourite of the monks of Evesham. After the battle, what was left of his body was taken by them to be buried before the high altar of their abbey church.

Very soon after his death, a spring broke out, bubbling up through the earth of the battlefield. The very place where he had fallen to the ground now offered up cooling water for weary men to drink. Furthermore, these waters were soon found to have healing properties. For this miracle the monks of Evesham Abbey gave due thanks, and Simon de Montfort's reputation as an unofficial saint began to grow. Though the site is now abandoned and weed-filled, until a century ago the waters which flowed from this spring were well known to be a certain cure for any eye complaint.

However, the most remarkable sign of Simon de Montfort's blessed status was the 'mensuratus', a piece of cord which had been used by his friends the monks to measure the length of his body in preparation for his burial. It soon became clear that this length of cord had powerful healing properties, as the story of a certain constable, William Child, demonstrates.

William Child, being a staunch supporter of the ruling monarch, King Henry III, was a sworn enemy of Simon de Montfort. Furthermore, de Montfort had earned Child's enmity by confiscating some property that had belonged to the constable. There was therefore no love lost between the two men, and William Child did not grieve when news reached him that his enemy was dead, slain in the battle against King Henry.

Soon after the Battle of Evesham and de Montfort's death, people realised that there were healing powers in the dead Earl's remains. Pilgrims began to make their way to the abbey church, to ask for help and the blessing of the bones buried beneath the altar.

One day, on returning home from the King's court, William Child was horrified to find that his son, his only son, his greatly loved young son, was gravely sick. The boy lay at death's door, and his father could think of no way to save his child. He prayed, and he went to the church and asked the help of the priest.

The priest listened and at last spoke to the distraught father, suggesting that he forget his anger against de Montfort and pray to the dead Earl of Leicester. With a certain shame and misgiving, Child knelt at the foot of the altar where the bones were buried and prayed. Prayed hard. But to no avail; perhaps he did not pray with sufficient ardour, for the boy died that very evening.

Overwhelmed with grief, and angry to have been fed false hope by the priest, the father stormed back to the abbey church and there he gave vent to his despair and anger. An old monk, seeing his distress, begged to know the cause of such great grief. Hearing how the father had prayed for help from the dead Earl, and that it had been in vain, quite useless, the monk shook his head. Then he reached into a small shelf beneath the altar, brought out the mensuratus, knelt beside the distraught father and waited. Gradually William Child ceased his wild outpourings of despair and gave heed to the gentle voice of the monk. The old monk spoke of the power contained within the fine thread of the cord that had been used to measure Simon de Montfort's dead body, and told the grieving father what he should do. 'You must take this blessed piece of cord and wrap it around your son's body. At the same time, you must pray for help from the dead Earl.'

Having listened to the monk and understanding the instructions, Child hurried back to his son's bedside. There he saw the white face of his son, felt the cold hand of death upon the boy's brow and wept more tears. And so many were his tears, so heavy his grief, that now Child felt an immense weariness creep over him. His eyes closed and he slept. He slept until in his dreams he heard a voice. It was the voice of Jesus, and Jesus said, 'Whatsoever you ask of me in the name of the Earl, it shall be given.'

William Child awoke, awoke with fresh hope, and did as he had been instructed. He wrapped the blessed cord around the boy and prayed for the life of his son, asked this of the lord Jesus, in the name of Simon de Montfort, Earl of Leicester. Then he waited. It was not long before the boy's cheeks showed a gentle flush; he stirred and opened his eyes to see his father, who was weeping now with joy, with relief.

For many years thereafter, the ordinary folk of the land continued to visit both the spring and the abbey church, asking for help and healing from this most unlikely of saintly beings. The people of Leicester, however, did have some tangible, material benefits to thank him for; he had 'remitted and quit-claimed for ever' both the tax levied on the timber brought in from the forests over Leicester's bridges, and the tax known as 'gable pence'. He had also given the people of the town an area of common land, for 'their use and occupation for ever'. To this gift we probably owe the open space we know as Victoria Park. He remains today a reminder of the city's past, our history. A street, a concert hall and a university all bear the name de Montfort.

2

MORE GOSSIP

Trickery, deception, 'getting one over' on those in authority –
what more apt, more pleasing, a subject for an evening session
of gossip around the fire?

PARSON PIKE

In the early part of the eighteenth century, Squire Thomas
Tooley and his wife, Emma, lived at Tooley Hall near Groby.
The squire was particularly friendly with James Pike, the rector
of Ratby. Both men had a lively sense of humour and a great
love of hunting, shooting and fishing. It was this love of sport
that led them to spend a lot of time together.

The squire had a small boat which they would row out
onto Groby Pool. After a good day's fishing they liked nothing
better than to return to Tooley Hall to enjoy the results of
their labours, for the squire's cook was particularly skilful in
producing fine fish dishes.

To see the two men together was a remarkable sight because
they were so different. The squire was only just of average

height, slight and wiry in build, though quite handsome of face. The parson, on the other hand, was over 6ft tall, weighed more than 18 stone, and in motion was rather like a lumbering carthorse. And he had a face that only his mother could ever describe as more than homely.

As well as those he shared with the rector, Squire Tooley had another more personal interest. He was used to being admired by young women because of his good looks and wealth, and he liked sporting with these pretty creatures almost as much as he liked hunting, shooting and fishing. He had become enamoured of a beautiful young woman. After a time of courting her with gifts, he took her as his mistress and set her up in a comfortable house in Ratby.

At this time, Parson Pike began to notice that their fishing trips had dwindled in frequency and that he was not invited to eat at the hall so often. This upset the clergyman, as he liked spending time in good company eating good food. His housekeeper just didn't have the skills of the cook at Tooley Hall.

Parson Pike's housekeeper did, however, have real skill in collecting gossip, and in due course she took great pleasure in passing on to the parson the juicy titbit that the squire 'has set up his fancy piece in a house in Ratby and that was why he is seen so often in the village'.

Parson Pike was now faced with a dilemma. Loyal to his friend, he was also very fond of the squire's wife, Emma, who always treated him so well on his visits. The rector obviously had to adhere to the rules and be seen to uphold the morality of society. He desperately tried to find a way to get his friend to mend his ways, and preached some sermons on the theme 'the Wages of Sin'. Nothing seemed to have any effect. Finally the parson felt that he had no alternative but to tell the squire's wife about the mistress established in the house in Ratby.

Soon after Parson Pike's visit to Emma at Tooley Hall, it was noticed that the squire had lost the spring in his step and his usual sunny face was decidedly cloudy. The parson's housekeeper relayed the information that 'the fancy piece' was no longer resident in the fine house in Ratby.

Now Parson Pike was certain that his times hunting and fishing with his friend, and the meals in good company, would be a thing of the past. Imagine then his surprise when, after the Sunday service, the squire approached him in his usual friendly way and invited him to go out fishing the next day.

The day dawned bright and sunny. The two men agreed to try their luck on Groby Pool and the squire rowed with great vigour and enthusiasm. They soon reached the centre of the pool. Suddenly and unexpectedly, Squire Tooley stood up and started to rock the small boat. Parson Pike tried desperately to hold on to the sides but because of his unwieldy bulk he lost his balance, slipped and tumbled over the side. Panicking and spluttering, he was deposited in the deep, cold water!

Fortunately the squire had several of his servants strategically placed around the pool and, using ropes and nets, they dragged the waterlogged 18 stone of parson out onto dry land. Once he had controlled his laughter and wiped the tears from his eyes, Squire Tooley turned to his men and said, 'Well done! That's definitely the biggest pike that'll ever come out of Groby Pool!' What Parson Pike said is not recorded.

THE LEICESTER CHAMBERMAID

Jack was a butcher. He lived with his father in London and together they made a good living, supplying the best cuts of meat to wealthy families of the town. To keep ahead of their rivals in the trade they needed to acquire some of the new breed of longhorn cattle which had been developed in Leicestershire by a certain Robert Bakewell. To that end, Jack was despatched to the cattle market in the town of Leicester.

Jack was a well set-up young fellow – handsome, with blue eyes and curly, golden hair. He fancied himself as a wheeler-dealer and took great pleasure in persuading the 'country yokels', as he called them, to sell their animals for a bargain price. His day at Leicester market went well. He had worked his 'bargaining magic', bought at a good price and felt well pleased with himself. He had entrusted the cattle to his drovers and then headed into town. Jack booked a room in one of the best inns, the Queens, in the town centre. It was an establishment he thought appropriate to his London status. He had worked hard, had money in his pocket and now deserved some entertainment.

That evening Jack was tucking into a good tripe supper, a feast for which the Queens was rightly famed. While downing his third pint of the local brew, he listened to the conversation around him. There was the usual talk of deals made at the cattle market, grumbles about increased taxes and, of course, tales of which serving girls would be willing to keep a man's bed warm, if the fee was right. It seemed to be agreed that just about all the young women were willing and available for the right price, all except young Bella. Bella was the niece of the landlord and moreover she was new both to Leicester and the work of serving in a busy town hostelry. It was readily and noisily agreed by all the clientele that Bella was 'a snooty little piece, who considered herself above the reach of mere market traders'. Anyway, woe betide any man who tried his luck with her, as her uncle was a big beefy man, rather quick of temper and heavy of hand. For Jack this was a challenge to which he must rise (as you might say)!

Later that evening, as the room was beginning to clear, Jack approached Bella. She was easily the prettiest girl he had seen all evening, with dark curls framing a lovely face and skin like peaches and cream. He could see straightaway that she too was impressed by his looks. His bright blonde hair was clean and shone in the firelight. Jack's fashionable London clothes and his speech and manners were so different from the bumbling market traders who usually frequented her uncle's inn. It took only a little flattery from Jack, a few tales of his extensive travels and the casual mention of wealthy parents to convince young Bella that this young buck was all she had ever dreamed of. And he was offering her a whole sovereign for what the other girls gave for a handful of small change. What harm could there be in spending the night with such a pleasant young man? Anyway, perhaps he would be so smitten by her charms that he would marry her and carry her back to London with him! And so the bargain was made and a pleasant night was spent by both parties.

In the early hours of the morning, Jack quietly gathered up his belongings and made his careful way downstairs. He needed to make an early start on his long journey back to London. Unfortunately for Jack it wasn't quite early enough. The landlord was already about. The big man filled the doorway and there was no way round him.

'Young man,' he bellowed, 'you haven't paid your bill!'

Jack opened his bright blue eyes and assumed an innocent expression, 'Oh, my dear sir,' he sputtered, 'I gave your maid, Bella, a whole sovereign, slipped it into her very own hand. Though the wench has still not given me my change. But I haven't time to wait any longer as my father expects me back by noon and I'm always obedient to that dear man.'

The landlord, completely taken in by the innocent-looking youth, called Bella down to explain herself. Jack watched as Bella reluctantly handed the gold sovereign to the landlord. It was hers by right, but how would she explain that to her uncle? She couldn't possibly say that the young man owed for some extra 'comforts' as well as for the tripe supper and night's lodging. What could she say of the night's doings?

Pretending unconcern Jack turned away, straightening his cap as he tried to listen to what Bella was whispering into her uncle's ear. Whatever her explanation, it seemed to satisfy the landlord, who, with profuse apologies, offered the change from the sovereign. But Jack, with a lordly shake of his head, waved aside the money, said 'Goodbye', and set off home with a light heart and a spring in his step. He was well content with his bargain.

Twelve months later Jack was again sent to Leicester to buy cattle for his father. This time the town was much busier and Jack could find only one room – at the very same Queens. He was not sure this was a good idea but, after all, what could a mere chambermaid do to him? No one would listen to her and if they did they'd think her no better than he. Jack was well into his third pint, and there was very little of his excellent tripe supper left, when he became aware of a buzz of expectation around him in the room.

There at his side appeared the buxom Bella, and in her arms a babe of about three months. This child she promptly plonked on Jack's knee!

'What's this?' asked Jack, open-mouthed and staring at the child.

'Kind sir, do not think it strange. One whole sovereign you gave to me and here I've brought your change!'

The room erupted with pleasure at Bella's cleverness.

Before long the story had spread throughout the town and was so popular that it was made into a broadside. And this broadside was read and enjoyed for many years, wherever there were handsome young women and lively young blades gathered together to hear the tale of the Leicester chambermaid.

So all you brisk and lively blades I pray be ruled by me,
And look well into your bargains before you money pay;
Or soon perhaps your folly will give you cause to range,
For when you sport with pretty maids be sure you'll get your change!

THE RAM JAM INN

The Great North Road, or A1 as it is now more generally known, runs through the county of Rutland on its way between Stamford and Grantham. About halfway along that stretch is the village of Stretton. It is there that the Ram Jam Inn, once called the Winchelsea Arms, can be found. A hundred miles from London, it was an important staging post on the way north. Many travellers have broken their journey there, and some may well have been 'gentlemen of the road', or highwaymen such as Dick Turpin who, they say, stayed at the inn on occasion. This story, however, is not about him but another unknown highwayman. It may well have happened in Turpin's time, or perhaps a little later, for it is not known exactly when the inn changed its name from the Winchelsea Arms to the Ram Jam Inn.

It happened one evening that a certain travel-stained stranger arrived at the inn and, having left his horse with the ostler, asked for a room. He would be wanting the room for the whole week. It being agreed, he immediately began to chat to the landlord, while the landlady organised a room for him – one of the best, as was desired by the gentleman.

The landlord found him a very pleasant fellow indeed, as did many of the other customers at the inn. As the week went by, however, they noticed that he was somewhat shabbily dressed, and didn't seem to have much spare cash. But his horse was a fine animal, and he got on well with everyone, being friendly and good humoured. He spent a lot of time chatting with all and sundry, about a host of different subjects, though he never seemed to reveal very much about himself. But he kept everybody well entertained, ate and drank well, and had everything put on his account.

On the last evening of his stay, after most people had departed for their beds or their homes, the gentleman was sat having a last drink and a chat with the landlord, while the landlady was washing up the pots in the back. He asked the landlord if he'd ever seen mild and strong ale taken from the same barrel. The landlord laughed at that and said, 'Don't be ridiculous, that's absolutely impossible.'

'No, really!' said the gentleman. 'It can be done, and in fact I could show you how, if you've got the time before I go.'

Well the landlord really laughed at that, and said, 'Pull the other leg, it's got bells on!'

The gentleman just smiled and shortly after retired to his room. Then, while they were doing the final clear up before going to bed, the landlord laughingly told his wife what the gentleman had said, and then thought no more about it.

His wife, though, thought considerably about it. 'Only think of the time and trouble it would save,' she told herself. 'We'd only need to bring one barrel up instead of two. It would take only half the effort required at present, and we'd have so much more room behind the bar.' It all sounded so wonderful, that she decided there and then that she would get the gentleman to show her how to do it before he left the inn.

The next day the landlord set off early in the morning to go to Stamford on business. He left his wife in charge of the inn for the day, as he was not expecting to be back before late afternoon. A little later that morning, the gentleman asked the landlady for his bill, and called for the ostler to ready his horse. The landlady then asked him if it was true that he knew how to get two sorts of beer from the same barrel.

'Oh, indeed I do,' smiled the man, 'and if you have the time now before I leave, I could show you at once.'

Well of course she had time! She was eager to find out all there was to know about this amazing trick.

'Right,' he said. 'If you'll find me some tools to put holes into the barrel, I'll just put my saddlebags onto my horse.'

So the tools were found, and down into the cellar they went, choosing the largest barrel there. The landlady, breathless with excitement, waited for him to start. Well, first he bored a hole low down on one side of the barrel.

'Quick,' he said, 'ram your thumb in there before we lose any of the ale.'

The landlady did as she was told, and then watched as he made another hole on the other side of the barrel.

'Now,' he said, 'jam your other thumb in there. Can you reach?'

She could – just. So there she was, stretched right across the barrel, her arms reaching down the curving sides with her thumbs rammed and jammed into the two holes. It was at this point that the gentleman 'discovered' that they didn't have any bungs or spile pegs handy to fit in the holes.

'Goodness me, we've forgotten the spile pegs,' he said. 'I'll just pop upstairs to the bar to fetch some. I won't be a moment.' He shot off up the stairs, before she'd even time to open her mouth. Then, closing the cellar door very quietly, he left the inn, and sauntered across the stable yard. He mounted his horse, tipped the ostler, rode out onto the Great North Road and was soon well away.

The landlady meanwhile was stretched out in a very awkward position, and dared not take her thumbs out of the holes in the barrel for fear of losing all that beer. At first she was a little uneasy, but she was becoming increasingly anxious, as it was taking far too long for him to find the spile pegs. Her arms and her hands were painfully cramped, and now she was angry as she realised that she had been tricked. She called; she shouted; she screamed and yelled for help; but it was some considerable time before anyone heard her and came to the rescue.

Just in time the beer was saved, but the landlady was aching and exhausted from her ordeal and upset into the bargain. She questioned the ostler, who told her that the gentleman had left some time ago.

'He's probably halfway to Stamford by now Missus. Why, is anything wrong?'

'Wrong! Wrong! He's only left without paying his bill!' she wailed. 'And I don't know how I'm going to tell my husband!'

From that day on, they say, the Winchelsea Arms has been known as the Ram Jam Inn, and for many years had a painted inn sign showing the landlady stretched across a large barrel, with her thumbs rammed and jammed into the holes on either side.

This is the most colourful of the stories attached to the name of this inn. The alternative version is a little more prosaic. In the nineteenth century, to 'ram jam' meant to stuff yourself with food, whilst inns and other buildings that were 'ram jam full' were filled to overflowing with people. This, of course, could indicate the popularity of a place and the generous amounts of food available.

Yet another story tells us of a publican in the mid-eighteenth century, Charles Blake by name. He is said to have brought from India a secret recipe for a rare and delicious, and extremely potent, liqueur. This he decided to name after his Indian servant, his 'ram jam'. He made up a quantity of this special drink and it became very popular; so popular, that he began to bottle it and sell it to his customers at the inn. As people frequently took their bottles to various destinations and shared them with friends, the popularity of the liqueur spread. People travelling the Great North Road began to look out for the inn that sold this wonderful drink. They were soon calling it The Inn That Sells Ram Jam, and when the landlord hung an advertising sign over the door to catch the passing trade, it readily became known as the Ram Jam Inn and folks forgot that it was really the Winchelsea Arms. Charles Blake, however, kept the secret of the recipe, and took it with him to the grave. So no one has been able to reproduce it since that time.

SWIFT NICK NEVISON

Did you ever hear tell of that hero
Bold Nevison it was his name
For he rode about like a brave hero
And by that he gained a great fame.

Bold Nevison was sometimes referred to as John, and sometimes as William, and was born roundabout 1640 in the county of Yorkshire. In his early teens he took to a life of crime, and, after stealing some money and a horse, he made his getaway to London.

His life was a colourful one, including highway robbery and thieving. He enlisted as a mercenary with the army in Flanders. He was even transported to a penal colony in Tangier, and managed to escape. But he was said to be very gallant to the ladies, and never used violence on his victims. He even had, like Robin Hood, a reputation for stealing from the rich and giving to the poor.

Now when I rode on the highway
I always had money in store
And whatever I took from the rich
Why I freely gave it to the poor.

Many of his victims were pursued along the Great North Road, where it passes through Rutland. He became a regular terror of the road, extracting protection money from the carters and drovers as they plied their business.

He was, however, most famous for two exploits. The first was the famous ride which was later mistakenly ascribed to Dick Turpin. In 1676 he robbed a man in Kent at 4 a.m. in the early dawn, then crossed the Thames, galloped through Cambridgeshire and up the Great North Road, arriving in York at 8 p.m. – having gone a distance of 200 miles. In York he immediately set about establishing an alibi with the Lord Mayor. His alibi was accepted by a jury, who could not believe that anyone could cover that distance in so short a time.

This incredible feat was soon widely spoken of; and it is said that King Charles II then dubbed him 'Swift Nick', for 'such speed could only have been achieved with the help of Old Nick himself'. Others said that his name came from the devilish speed with which, on several occasions, he got himself out of jail.

Swift Nick's other most famous exploit was his escape from Leicester Jail. He had strayed away from the Great North Road and into Leicestershire, where he committed several robberies. He was finally caught and taken to Leicester Jail in High Cross Street. Because of his reputation, he was kept under heavy guard at all times, and was put into manacles and leg irons and kept chained up to ensure that he couldn't escape.

No sooner was he incarcerated, than he began to plot his escape. First he got rid of the leg irons that restricted his movements. Next it seemed that his best bet would be to feign some illness, so he set about deceiving the jailor by an elaborate charade of moans and groans. So convincing was Swift Nick's performance that very soon he had the jailer believing in this illness, and three of his best cronies were allowed to visit him. One of them, impersonating a doctor, immediately confirmed the diagnosis: a dreadful illness which could only be cured if the prisoner were to be given better quarters. 'Where there's some fresh air and he'll sleep easier,' he said. As the jailer was afraid of losing the prisoner to illness, thus denying the public the spectacle of a hanging, he unlocked all the chains and had Nevison carried to a much brighter room with a proper window and a bed.

The 'doctor' visited a second time and announced that the prisoner was much worse, and that he was probably highly contagious. This made the jailer's wife panic, and she stopped her husband from getting any nearer to Nevison than the doorway to his cell. Nor would she let any of the servants enter into the prisoner's cell. This, of course, was just what the schemers had hoped for.

The third time the 'doctor' came he brought some paints. As the staff at the jail were keeping well away from the 'infected' man, he was able to paint some very artistic plague spots upon the prisoner. He also gave Nick a very strong sleeping draught, so that soon he lay in a coma-like sleep. The jailer was then informed that Swift Nick was dead of the plague. Once he had seen the dreaded plague spots (from the doorway of course) and the apparently lifeless corpse, the jailor was only too pleased to have the body removed at once, for fear of contagion.

Nevison's trusty friends protected themselves from the 'plague' by masks, brought a coffin into the prison and laid him in it. Then they nailed the lid on tight and carried it out of the jail. Carted away to a safe haven, Swift Nick was finally released from his imprisonment.

Swift Nick soon returned to his extortion racket along the Great North Road. The drovers and carters and his other victims had all heard reports of his death in prison, so naturally they thought it must be the ghost of Swift Nick come back to rob them, just as he had done in life. Only gradually did it dawn on folk that if it was not his ghost, then it must surely be Old Nick himself! Finally they realised that a great trick had been played, and the law had been well and truly cheated by an all-too-living Swift Nick Nevison.

> I have never robbed no man of tuppence
> And I've never done murder nor killed
> Though guilty I've been all my lifetime
> So gentlemen do as you will.

HIGH COCKALORUM

The cobbler sat in his workshop with a shoe on the last in front of him, showing his apprentice how to put a new sole on. After a while, his apprentice said, 'Why do you call yourself a cobbler on the sign outside?'

The cobbler took some nails out of his mouth. 'Because that's what I am.'

'But it's so old-fashioned,' said the lad.

'It's a very old trade, and I'm proud of it.'

'Well it sounds a bit common and boring; all my friends say so! Why don't you call yourself a 'Shoe Repairer' or a 'Footwear Specialist'? That would sound much grander.'

'Sounding grander is not always better,' answered the cobbler. 'Did you never hear tell of High Cockalorum?'

'High Cockalorum! What's that?'

'It's what they call high footling speech, or a self-important man who likes to call everything by fancy names,' said his master. 'And as I heard it, it didn't do the man in the tale any good at all.'

'It didn't? Why was that then?' The apprentice shuffled into a comfy position in anticipation of a good story.

'Very well, I'll tell you, as I see I shall get no peace until I do,' and, putting his hammer down, the cobbler began the story, the story of the old gentleman who insisted on his grandson calling him Door Perceptor instead of Grandpa.

The grandson, stroking the cat, asked, 'Door Perceptor, what is pussy called?'

'That's not Pussy,' said the old man. 'That's White-faced Sympathy.'

'All right,' said the boy. Looking at the fire, which was getting low, he then asked, 'Shall I make the fire up, Door Perceptor?'

'Indeed you can but you must always call it High Cockalorum; do try and remember that, there's a good lad; and you should call the chimney the Hyper-Mount. Now if you would like some tea, you can put the kettle on.'

Well the boy thought that would be nice, so, after mending the fire, he picked up the kettle, and asked where he could find some water.

'Not water boy, you must call it Absolution! There's a drop in that bucket over there; there should be enough for a cuppa.'

'Righty-ho,' said the lad, and, having filled the kettle, he put it on the hob to boil. 'What about these trousers hanging here; I think they've dried now?'

'Trousers, boy, trousers? Those are my Fire Crackers; give them to me and I'll take them up the Mountain Pass there, as now I'm going to, to …'

'To bed?' interrupted the boy.

'No, no, no! It's not bed, it's Lazy Decree!' shouted his grandfather.

'Oh! Very well,' said his grandson, 'I'll try to remember; and I'll come up after I've had my cup of tea. Goodnight Door Perceptor.'

Well, the boy sat by the hearth waiting for the kettle to boil, and while he was waiting he gave the fire a good poke. But, no sooner had he done so, a cinder flew out and fell onto the cat's back. The cat leapt into the air, and darted to and fro in a mad fright, and then shot up the chimney in total panic. The boy ran to the foot of the stairs and, after some thought, shouted up to his grandfather, 'Door Perceptor! Door Perceptor! Get out of your Lazy Decree; put on your Fire Crackers and come down Mountain Pass. White-faced Sympathy has gone up Hyper-Mount with High Cockalorum on its back; and if you don't come down and get some Absolution to throw on it, then everything will be destroyed.'

The cobbler was shouting by the time he got to the end of his story, and his apprentice, watching him solemnly, asked, 'And then what happened?'

'Well,' said the cobbler, 'by the time his grandson had remembered all those fancy names and had finished saying all that, the chimney and half of the thatched roof was burning fast; and so the old man was lucky to escape from the fire wearing only his nightshirt!'

The Ballad of the Oakham Poachers

Sometimes, of course, the authorities win.

In the eighteenth and nineteenth centuries, the enclosure of common land was speeding up. Private landlords were taking over these lands and the poor people, who were used to helping out their household economy with an occasional rabbit or pheasant, bitterly resented the process. This was particularly harsh in the Midlands, where something like a guerrilla war developed between gamekeepers and so-called poachers.

This song, located in Rutland, is one of many in which all sympathy is on the side of the alleged lawbreakers. It appeared on several broadsides by London, Midland and Northern publishers. It tells of three brothers, John, Robert and George Perkins; one was fatally shot by keepers and the other two were hanged for their crime.

This version, as sung by John Kirkpatrick, is from a singer named Goliath Cole. The words are partly Goliath's and partly taken from the singing of Wiggy Smith, a Gipsy singer.

Young men of every station, that dwell within this nation,
Pray hear my lamentation, a sad and mournful tale.
Concerning of three fine young men that lately were confined
And heavily bound in irons in Oakham county gaol.

It was on last February, against our laws contrary
Three brothers quite unwary of a-poaching went, we hear.
To Oakham Woods they rambled, through briars and through brambles,

And they fired at pheasants random, till it brought the keepers near.

Those keepers did not enter, nor dared those woods to venture
But outside and near the centre, an ambush they did lie
As homeward they were making, nine pheasants they were taking
Until the keepers faced them and they saw that they should die.

Well these brothers being brave hearted, they boldly kept on firing
Till one of them got the fateful blow and they were overthrown
As he lay there a-crying, like one who was a-dying
With no assistance neigh him, his blood in streams did flow.

May He who feeds the raven, grant these men peace in Heaven.
And their sins may be forgiven, ere they resign their breath;
For to gaol they quick were taken, so cruelly were they beaten.
Till the judge he guilty found them and he sentenced them to death.

So come all young men take warning and don't the laws be scorning

For in our day just dawning, we're cut off in our prime

And all you jolly poachers that hear of we three brothers

It's for our brother's sake makes our hearts ache and then with us to die.

(Traditional)

3

THE UNEXPLAINED

The Guildhall has its fair share of ghostly inhabitants, unexplained noises and sudden drifts of cold air; an agitated black phantom hound lopes around the courtyard, and a ghostly black cat races up and down the stairs leading from the Great Hall up to the Recorder's bedroom and the Old Town Library.

There is also the White Lady. She haunts the library, where the King James I Bible is left open at a verse from Proverbs: 'A word fitly spoken is like apples of gold in pictures of silver.' (Proverbs, Chapter 25) Curiously, when the building is empty overnight, a spectral hand will sometimes turn the pages of the Holy Book to leave it open at a different passage. The White Lady, whose name is believed to be Mary, perhaps?

It is not surprising that staff at the Guildhall have had some disturbing experiences. After closing one evening, the CCTV suddenly showed someone in the library. About to leave for home, Oriana hurried up the stairs to confront the intruder, only to find the room empty. Empty, that is, except for a pair of ghostly child's legs standing beside the library chair. There was no visible body in the room.

FOUR EGGS A PENNY

Tom was a very poor fellow, though not as poor as the old beggar man Joe. Joe had absolutely nothing. Despite this, Tom and the beggar man often spent time together, and Tom was well entertained by the beggar man, for Joe had a fund of jokes and merry tales, tales which he was only too happy to tell in exchange for a bite to eat.

Now, to earn a little money, Tom searched for eggs in the hedgerows and woodlands. Any eggs found, he took to Oakham to sell on market days. A single egg found and then sold earned Tom a farthing, and for four eggs he got a whole penny. In those days you could buy a surprising amount of things for a penny. Whenever Tom managed to find two or more eggs, he would leave one on the window sill for the old beggar man Joe to enjoy.

One market day Tom thought himself very lucky, for he had found several nests, and had two dozen eggs to take to market. He was looking forward to the silver sixpence he could get for them.

'I'll be able to buy a whole loaf,' said Tom to himself.

But then he remembered the poor beggar man and the single egg he was in the habit of leaving for him, whenever he had more than one to sell.

'Oh well,' said Tom, 'I can still get a good piece of bread and maybe some butter to go on it, for my five pence three farthings. If Joe comes by when I get back home again, then we'll have a real feast, and he'll make me laugh, and it will be a grand evening.'

So, as usual, he left one egg for old Joe, and off he went to market with his twenty-three eggs. Having been fortunate at the market, selling every one of his eggs, he set off for home with five whole pennies and three small farthings in his trouser pocket. However, when he got home, he was shocked to see the old beggar man lying in the road outside the alehouse. On investigation, poor old Joe was found to be dead. This was most upsetting. What was even worse was the reaction of the alewife when Tom asked her for help.

'He can lie in the dirt for all I care,' she said. 'He owed me a penny, and now I shall never get it back from him.'

Well Tom couldn't bear that, so he gave the alewife one penny to cancel Joe's debt. Then he searched in his pockets for two halfpennies to lay on the old man's eyelids. These were to pay St Peter when Joe arrived at the gates of heaven.

After that he went to the carpenter to get a coffin to put the corpse in. That cost him one whole penny and a halfpenny, the price of six eggs. But a farmer, seeing his plight, kindly helped Tom load the dead man and the coffin onto his cart and drove them to the parson. The farmer did it for nothing but Tom's grateful thanks.

'The old man made me merry many's the time,' the farmer said. Tom said the same, and they shared some of their memories on their way to the parson.

Unfortunately the parson and the clerk were not so amenable, not so charitable. They took all the rest of Tom's money – two pennies and the last little farthing – before they would bury the old beggar man. And even then they would only agree to put the old man in the darkest corner of the north side of the churchyard. Finally, having seen his friend Joe laid to rest, Tom said a quiet prayer for his soul, and went home as hungry as he'd come.

'No bread and butter for me today,' he said. 'There's just one potato in the cupboard. I'll have to tighten my belt.'

But when he arrived home, what a surprise he had. There was a nice warm fire waiting for him, and laid out all ready on the table was a large, fresh loaf of crusty bread, a beautiful pat of butter, and a basket containing twenty-four eggs! He couldn't believe it at first. Where had they come from? Who had put them there? It was like a miracle!

Then he noticed that the egg which he had left that morning on the window sill for Joe was gone. Now Tom understood that this feast, laid in his own house, must be thanks from a grateful soul, and he knew that it truly was a miracle.

RICHARD SMITH – SADDLER

Young Richard Smith, a well-respected saddler of Hinckley town, just twenty years of age, was often to be seen striding through the marketplace in his good brown broadcloth coat and shiny brown boots, smiling broadly at friends and acquaintances. One morning in early spring, as he came down Duckpuddle Lane, he came upon a crowd of his fellow townspeople, gathered around the old oak tree. They were listening to a man in a scarlet tunic: the recruiting sergeant.

The sergeant was brandishing his halberd (a long lance-like weapon) whilst haranguing the crowd. The audience shuddered as he reminded them of the fate which awaited all England should the Scots and James Stuart be victorious. He was in the middle of a rant about 'Papists ruling the land, torturing and burning people in the marketplace', when Richard interrupted, shouting out that 'Not all Catholics were that bad'.

The sergeant's face grew red; he turned on the heckler. 'You, sir, should don the scarlet and fight for the King. I warrant

that like every other man in this town you drink in the public house, the George. And what is the pub named after but our King George, God save his Majesty?'

Richard, unable to contain himself, contradicted the sergeant, saying, 'Everyone knows that the inn was named after St George that killed the dragon, not for any fat Hanoverian king.' Seeing the sergeant made to look a fool for his ignorance, the crowd began to jeer and laugh at him. This infuriated the soldier. He turned on Richard and drove his weapon at him, thrusting the halberd straight through the saddler's body, pinning him to the tree.

Horrified, the crowd scattered. Some went for the doctor, others to fetch Richard's parents. By the time they had returned the sergeant had vanished and escaped capture, for a horse can very soon be gone on good roads.

Richard Smith's body was taken down from the tree and now lay cold and dead beneath it; dead for making a joke at the expense of the recruiting sergeant.

Since that time, every April when the trees were turning green, friends of Richard visited his grave. And they swore that, as they stood there watching, great drops of blood-red moisture bubbled up through the cold grey stone, and lay glistening upon the gravestone. On this headstone the following words are inscribed:

A fatal halberd then his body slew
The murdering hand God's vengeance shall pursue.
From earthly shades, though justice took her flight,
Shall not the Judge of all the World do Right?

THE WITCHES OF BELVOIR

The courtroom at Lincoln Assizes was completely silent. It was as though everyone there was afraid even to breathe. All eyes were turned to watch Joan Flower as she raised a small piece of bread to her mouth. Would they finally know whether she was guilty of the terrible crimes of which she was accused?

It had all started eight years earlier, in 1611. King James was on the throne and he was fascinated by tales of witchcraft and magic. He had even written a book about it. It was a fascination and a fear shared by most of his subjects.

In Langham, in the county of Rutland, lived a woman called Joan Flower. Joan, although poor, had gained herself some standing in her village and surrounding area by openly declaring herself a witch. She boasted of performing deeds of Black Magic with the help of her Rutterkin, her mangy black cat familiar.

Joan had set herself up as head of a small coven of witches, with her two daughters and three other local women.

Between them, the six women terrorised the locals and thus managed to get a comfortable living.

Joan's two daughters, Philippa and Margaret, were in the service of the Earl and Countess of Rutland, who lived at Belvoir Castle. Philippa helped in the nursery. Margaret had been a poultry keeper and laundress until she was caught pilfering eggs and was dismissed from the Earl's service. The Countess refused to give her a good character, without which Margaret would be unable to find employment with any other local dignitaries.

Joan was incandescent with rage at this treatment of her daughter, calling down curses on the Earl and Countess. In 1613 Joan decided to make an example of them so that everyone would know that it was not wise to cross her. With Ellen Green of Stathern, Joan Willimott of Goadby, Anne Baker of Bottesford, and her daughters, Margaret and Philippa, Joan climbed to the top of Blackberry Hill near Langham. This hill was well known to local people as a sinister place where Black Magic was practised. The women took their familiars with them. Once at the very top, they made a pact with the Devil that he would help them take revenge on the Earl and Countess and their three children.

Philippa had with her a glove belonging to Lord Ross, the young son of the Earl and Countess. Joan dipped this glove in boiling water, rubbed it along Rutterkin's back and then pricked it with pins. Just one week after this ceremony, the little boy sickened and died. Next they acquired a handful of feathers from a quilt belonging to the Earl and Countess. Joan boiled the feathers in water, mixed them with blood, and cursed the couple with sterility: 'May they have no more children.'

Anne Baker   Joane Willmoll   Ellen Greene

However, the death of the young Lord Ross was not enough vengeance for Joan and her coven. They met again, this time trying the same magic on the younger son, Francis. Soon this child also fell sick. However, he recovered. The angry witches then buried his glove in a dung heap, believing that as the glove decayed the child would fade away. At around the same time it was noticed that the daughter, Katherine, was also looking ill.

Strangely, the coven was not secretive about what they were doing and, as the children became sick, people grew ever more fearful of the six women. The Earl was convinced that someone was using evil spells against him and his family. He sent loyal servants to find out what they could. It wasn't long before word of Joan's boasting came to the castle.

At Christmas time in 1618 all six women were arrested. They were imprisoned in Lincoln Gaol. After questioning, the six women were brought before the Lincoln Assizes in 1619. Despite all the evidence and the witnesses to her previous boasting, Joan Flower now maintained that she was innocent. In court she demanded that bread be brought for her to eat.

'Surely,' she said, 'God will choke me on this bread if I am guilty!'

In the silent courtroom all eyes turned to watch Joan Flower as she put the bread in her mouth – and promptly choked and died!

The rest of the coven were found guilty. Joan's daughters were hanged; what happened to the others is not recorded. Unfortunately, the deaths of the witches did not save little Francis. He died in 1620. A sad memorial to the Earl and his family in Bottesford Church states:

> He had two sonnes, both which dyed in their infancy by wicked practice and sorcerye.

HARRY'S BUS

The bus company that previously ran the county services in Leicestershire was the Midland Red or, to give its full and grand title, the Birmingham & Midland Motor Omnibus Co. Ltd.

Back when our story begins, buses looked very different from today's. The passengers climbed aboard the bus at the back, where the conductor stood when not collecting fares. The driver had a separate cab at the front of the bus.

Conductors and drivers had regular routes; one conductor, Harry Gamble, along with his driver, ran the 616 service that started at St Margaret's Bus Station in the centre of Leicester, destination Uppingham, a small market town in Rutland. It stopped at numerous little villages along the way.

Harry, being a young man with an eye for the ladies, couldn't help but notice that a regular passenger was a pretty young lady who smiled at him shyly when he handed her a ticket. Eventually they exchanged a few words, and then one day when she boarded the bus, to Harry's delight, she sat on the seat just inside from the platform. When Harry was not collecting fares they were able to chat and he discovered that her name was Mary Quinn and that she lived with her parents in a cottage opposite the church in the main street of the village of Tugby, just off the road to Uppingham. Mary described her parents' cottage, telling him about the leaded glass in the blue front door surrounded by roses. Harry thought how wonderful it must be to live in such pleasant surroundings.

Harry was always delighted whenever Mary boarded his bus and, after they had been chatting for a few weeks, he thought he would pluck up the courage to ask her out. Next time Mary boarded his bus he planned to ask.

However, the chance didn't arise. As the bus left Leicester on what had been a warm summer day, storm clouds were gathering and, before they had passed the city boundary, large spots of rain appeared on the bus windows and the rumble of thunder could be heard in the distance. Before long the storm broke and torrential rain lashed down, slowing the bus to a crawl. Deafening claps of thunder rolled directly overhead and flashes of lightning momentarily lit up a dark, angry sky.

The bus arrived at Mary's village but all she was wearing was a pretty cotton summer dress. Harry was concerned that Mary would have to walk to her home through the storm dressed as she was. 'Look,' he said, 'I've got this old coat I keep for emergencies.'

Harry reached under the stairs and brought out an old grey jacket with a hood, far too big for Mary, but at least it would keep off most of the rain. Mary thanked him and pulled the coat around her, and the last he saw of her she was hurrying down the road holding the hood in place over her head.

Over the next few days Harry kept a lookout for Mary, hoping that the next time she travelled on his bus he would at last be able to ask her out. A week – then two weeks – passed, and still no sign of Mary, which he found strange. Harry asked other conductors who also worked that route, but no one remembered seeing the young lady. He thought it odd. Surely she must have travelled on the days he was not working, and the other conductors must have noticed this pretty young woman. Why did she always travel at the same time, never talk to any of the other passengers and was only ever seen on the outward journey from Leicester?

After three weeks Harry became agitated and concerned about Mary's disappearance and decided it was time to try to find her. So, on his next day off, he boarded his regular bus as a passenger, intending to travel to Mary's village and look for her.

The conductor laughed when he saw Harry get on. 'What's this, a busman's holiday?' he asked. 'I don't suppose it's got anything to do with a certain young lady you've been asking about around the depot?'

Harry made no comment and sat quietly until the bus reached the stop where he had last seem Mary hurrying down the road wearing his old coat.

The village was exactly as Mary had described it and Harry walked down the main street until, opposite the church, he saw the cottage with the blue front door with leaded glass and roses growing on the trellis either side. Cautiously he knocked on the door, but no one came. Again he knocked, louder this time. He heard a bolt being pulled back and the door opened just a few inches, but enough for Harry to see an elderly woman.

'Excuse me,' said Harry. 'I'm looking for Mary, Mary Quinn.'

The woman made no reply and pushed the door shut. Harry thought that perhaps the woman had not heard him and decided to try once more with a loud knock. This time the door was not opened but the woman shouted, 'Go away, why are you tormenting us?'

Harry was not sure what to do next. This was definitely the right cottage, exactly as described by Mary. He looked along the street and saw, further down, a man tending his small front garden. Perhaps he could confirm he had the right cottage. Harry approached the man.

'Excuse me. I wonder if you could help me?' Harry enquired. 'I'm looking for a Mary Quinn. I've been to the cottage up there, but the old lady seemed to be upset by my visit.'

'Ahh,' the man replied, looking a little troubled. 'You'd better follow me lad.'

The man led Harry across the street to the church, then along a row of ancient gravestones, until they reached a newer part of the churchyard. There he stopped and looked down on a fairly recent gravestone. Harry was shocked to read the inscription: 'Mary Quinn a beloved daughter', and below this her date of birth followed by a second date. Harry stared at the inscription, unbelieving; the girl on his bus had been dead two whole years. Then he noticed something familiar. Hanging by its hood, at the back of the gravestone, was his old grey coat.

THE HAYMARKET AFFAIR

This tale was told to me some years ago by a library assistant at St Barnabas Library in Leicester. It was told to her by friends of the couple in question, or possibly by friends of her friends; I cannot be sure which now.

A couple had gone to see a show at the old Haymarket Theatre in the Haymarket Shopping Centre in Leicester. They had parked their car, an elderly model with shiny chrome bumpers, in the multi-storey car park there. Now, the Haymarket car park has an ill-lit and extremely convoluted layout, with many twists and turns, dead ends and dark corners. An eerie, frightening place, especially after nightfall.

After the show, they were making their way back to their car, when they saw a small group of youths. One of these lads had a length of chain and was wielding it like a whip, lashing out at the parked cars. Nervous now – indeed very frightened – they hurried to their car, clambered inside, locked the doors, and got the engine started. Suddenly, just as they were backing out from the parking bay, they saw the gang leader. He was directly behind them and hit out at the rear window of their car. They crashed into forward gear and drove off as fast as they dared, along the twisting turning route, round and round, spiralling down the circular ramp to the exit.

Still shaking from the shock of the attack, they pulled into their driveway, climbed out and staggered round to inspect the damage to the boot of the car, their pride and joy. They looked, and were horror-struck – not by the damage done to their car, bad as that was, but by the length of chain caught in the polished chrome bumper. Entangled in the chain were four bloody fingers.

Sickened, they went inside to phone the police. Soon a police car drove up and two policemen got out. Having taken photographs, they listened to the old couple's story and removed the evidence. The fingers went to the emergency department at the Leicester Royal Infirmary, and were reunited with their original owner. The youths were very soon arrested, charged with vandalism and sentenced, for the evidence of the fingers left them with not a leg to stand on!

THE GHOST OF BROOKSBY HALL

Brooksby Hall, near Melton Mowbray, was the home of the Villiers family from the thirteenth to the early eighteenth centuries. In 1592 it belonged to Sir George Villiers; at this time his son, also George, was born to his second wife. Very soon after the birth, the new mother realised that her child would have but a meagre inheritance to look forward to. Sir George had two older sons by his first wife; they were the only heirs to what was, at that time, a modest estate. So, when in 1604 Sir George died, his wife had her son educated for court.

George was a strikingly handsome young man, and when he was introduced at court in 1614 he caught the eye of King James I. The King immediately became quite besotted with him, and would hang his arms around George and slobber him with kisses, scandalising the courtiers. As the King's favourite, he was rapidly advanced from a mere knight through the ranks of the peerage to become a baron, then a viscount, a marquis, an earl, and finally the Duke of Buckingham. George now had riches and power and position, for in 1619 the King created him Lord High Admiral.

When James I died in 1625, George Villiers rapidly became the favourite of the next sovereign, King Charles I. Charles appointed him First Minister, though he had few of the skills needed for the position. His support for the High Church alienated the Puritans, and his policies as Lord High Admiral, especially the campaigns at Cadiz and in France, had enraged Parliament and proved disastrous. Hated by the people, he was yet a favourite amongst some of the court. Indeed, his greatest skill seems to have been the skill of being the 'favourite'.

It was in 1628, as Buckingham was planning a second expedition to France, that the ghost of his father, Sir George Villiers, made a visitation to an old servant. Parker was sat reading late one night. The candles guttered, the old man shivered, the book slid slowly to the floor. 'Parker,' whispered the apparition, 'Go to your master, go to the Duke, my son; urge him that he should abandon his plans. Tell him that he must avoid the company of a certain prominent person, lest he come to harm.' With that the spirit faded away, leaving Parker startled and confused, and convinced that he had fallen asleep over his book. It was just a dream, a dream to be ignored.

A second time the ghost appeared to Parker. This time it spoke more urgently, 'I charge you, old man, warn him, on no account to pursue his plans for an expedition to France. Tell the Duke that he should abandon Charles. Tell him that if he does not somewhat ingratiate himself with the people, or at least abate the extreme malice they have against him, he will be suffered to live but a short time. Befriend the people of this country. And no longer serve the King, lest he come to death and destruction.'

Now Parker had a problem; having encountered the ghost a second time he knew that it was no dream. The message was clear and very important. But how to convey this warning from beyond the grave to his master? The Duke was well known to be a sceptic, having no time for those who believed in ghostly visitations. Parker decided that it would be useless to even attempt to pass the warning to Buckingham, so he did nothing.

Then the apparition paid the old servant a third visit, demanding to know why he had failed to deliver the warning.

'Well, Your Lordship, the problem is this. The Duke, my master, will never believe me, seeing as he scoffs at all mention of ghosts and spirits coming back from the dead, begging your pardon sir, you being … er … a spirit so to speak.'

'Indeed, 'tis true old man, I do remember me of his unbelief. But, no matter; you shall confide this to him, a secret known only to him, to me and to his mother.' Parker felt the cold breath of a whispered word in his ear. Then he saw the ghost draw an incorporeal dagger from beneath its robe and hold it high, saying, 'Deliver this warning to the Duke; if he do not change his ways, death will most surely come for him. He will die by the dagger, and then, old man, you too will die, your death will follow close upon that of your master.' With these words the ghost of Sir George Villiers faded from sight. This proved to be its last message.

Parker now set off on the journey from Brooksby to London, to seek out the Duke of Buckingham. It was not easy to track down such a busy man, and even more difficult to get to speak privately with him, but he finally managed, thanks to the intervention of the Duke's mother. At first Buckingham was very sceptical about the whole affair, but when Parker revealed the closely guarded secret to him he was amazed, for none knew of it save his mother, her dead husband and himself. His mother soon swore that she most certainly had never revealed the secret to the old servant Parker.

Despite these warnings from beyond the grave, the Duke carried on with his plans for a second expedition against

France, and a few weeks later he was in Portsmouth to finalise preparations. He was at breakfast at the Greyhound inn, attended by a great company, when suddenly he was stabbed in the heart by a dagger. Vainly attempting to pull out the blade, he staggered forward a few paces, crying, 'The villain has killed me!' He then collapsed and died. Immediately there was confusion; at first it was thought that he had died of an apoplexy, but when the people saw the great pooling of blood it became clear that this was an assassination. In the great press of people at the inn, many thought this was a French plot, and swords were drawn, fearing further violence and more bloodshed.

Relative calm was only restored when the real assassin was revealed to be an officer called John Felton. He boldly stated that he had done the deed and was willing to sacrifice himself 'in God's honour', declaring, 'I am glad to have killed one who for so long has gone unpunished for his crimes.'

It was later revealed that Felton had fought and been wounded in one of Buckingham's disastrous and ill-planned campaigns. He had a second grievance, believing himself to have been wrongly passed over for promotion by Buckingham.

George Villiers, Duke of Buckingham, was buried in Westminster Abbey. The route to the abbey was lined by armed guards, ordered to protect the coffin from the exultant, cheering crowds. The old servant, Parker, who had tried in vain to persuade his master to change his ways, died shortly after the Duke, just as had been foretold by the ghost of Sir George Villiers.

4

WITCHES, GIANTS AND BOGEYMEN

BLACK ANNIS

It is almost axiomatic that the deities of conquered peoples survive as witches, devils or monsters of some kind. The Irish goddess Anu or Danu is no exception. Little is remembered of her in her ancient, primeval form, for we have no stories of her. She is, however, known to have been the mother of the gods of the Celts (the *Tuatha Dé Danann* – literally 'the people of Danann') and she does survive in the monstrous form of Black Annis, with her fearsome, long, iron claws, which she uses to tear her victims to pieces. Black Annis lives in a cave in the Dane Hills, a mile or so west of the city, in the rock carved out by her own sharpened talons. Sometimes she takes on her cat form as Cat Anna and prowls the night streets, hungry and searching for food. As the eighteenth-century poet John Heyrick Junior wrote:

'Tis said the soul of mortal man recoiled
To view Black Annis's eye, so fierce and wild.
Vast talons, foul with human flesh, there grew

In place of hands, and features livid blue
Glared in her visage; while the obscene waist
Warm sting of human victims close embraced

It has been suggested that her name is the root for the river names Danube, Don, and Dnieper, and possibly the Dane Hills in Leicester. It is said that she lurks in Rupert's Gateway, near Leicester Castle, waiting to drop down on unsuspecting and unaccompanied children.

In the time of the Normans, a great castle was built on a hill above a river. Peasants had laboured long under the eye of the master builder, till at last it was done. The King, his knights, and the great lords of that time, came, feasted and went hunting in the vast forests that lay beyond the river surrounding the castle.

Then they moved on to another castle and only the peasants, the poor people, were left – defenceless and at the mercy of bandits and robbers. But though they feared these wild bands of men, the peasants feared the witch that lived in the Dane Hills far more, for her skin was blue and her teeth were long and sharp and she ate people, especially children. And when she had sucked the blood from the flesh and the flesh from the bones, she hung up the skins to dry on a great oak tree that grew beside her cave. And they called her Black Annis. But sometimes she changed herself into a great black cat and went hunting. Then folk called her Cat Anna. And when they heard her howl as she roamed the hills, the poor folk in their hovels pulled the skins over the window openings, fastened the doors as best they could, and shivered.

In one of the huts, a poor woman lay dying. Three children knelt by her, her husband held her hand in his, and when all life had ebbed from her, he laid her body down and took from around her neck a leather thong threaded with a holed stone. 'Here,' he said to his eldest son, 'keep it – 'tis protection against evil. Look through the hole if ever you do fear danger.' And the family mourned the mother. But in time the man knew he must find help to care for his three sons, for they were very young, and a woman came to live with them. But she was thin and sharp, and nothing pleased her.

Annie Maiden of the well ;

As the boys grew she drove them to all the hardest, most disagreeable, tasks. And she gave them only the most meagre of scraps to eat.

On the afternoon of Halloween, that most dangerous of times, she drove them out into the bitter cold, screaming at them, 'Get wood, get wood, you worthless lot! Go, go, we need wood.' The three boys cowered in front of the woman and watched her shut the door against them. It was already late afternoon and would soon be dark; there was nothing for it, they must search for wood for the fire. They found some sticks hard by the castle walls, but they were few and small, for on the castle hill no trees grew. On the other side of the river the forest was thick; there would be plenty of firewood there.

'Come,' said Jem, the oldest, 'we'll have to go across.'

As they waded across the river, the boys knew that it would soon be that time when witches have most power.

'Quick! Get what wood we can here and leave it in a pile. Then we'll have to go further into the forest.'

'But Black Annis?'

'Shhh,' said Jem. 'She'll be in her cave for a while yet.'

So the boys went further and further into the forest, intent on their search for wood until, in the distance, they heard a howl.

'Black Annis,' said the littlest.

'No-n-no; a dog.'

'Look,' said John, the middle one, 'you've got our mother's stone. Quick – look through the hole.' And Jem, who'd forgotten all about it, took the stone from around his neck and looked. In the far, far distance, much farther away than he could have seen without the stone, he saw a figure with a blue face.

''Tis her, 'tis Black Annis, but she's a long way away; she'll not find us before we gets back safe. Our mother did tell me she don't see well.'

'But she can smell; she can smell the smell of us from ever so far. Look again Jem, through the hole.'

And Jem looked again, and saw the witch lift up her nose, and saw the flare of dark hairy nostrils. And then he saw her hoist her black skirts to her knees and start to run; she had caught wind of them.

'Quick, take little'un's hand and run!'

'What about firewood?'

'Leave it; drop it on the path. Happen she'll fall over it.'

They ran – they ran fast – but behind them was the sound of feet following. Every now and then those footsteps stopped and then they heard a deep snuffling.

'Faster, faster!' Jem urged John as they pulled and lifted little'un between them.

Suddenly they heard curses and a howling.

'She's fallen, tripped on that wood! She'll have to go back to get something to stop the blood; witches bleed ever so much.'

'Right,' said Jem, listening to the retreating footsteps, 'she's gone. We'd best get what wood we piled up before and get back home.' And though their hearts were still beating wildly, the boys felt safe now and gathered more wood.

Great piles they had in their arms as they came to the river, so that they did not notice the silent black shape that was slinking after them. They waded across the river. The cat waited, crouching, ready to spring. It leapt. Witches don't like water, nor do cats, but cats can jump. Cat Anna leapt onto a floating log, then onto an overhanging branch; a third mighty leap and she was on castle hill. Hearing the soft thud of the cat's landing, the boys turned and saw her. Then she pounced. They heard the sound of ripping flesh, cracking bones and a woman's scream. But they did not wait to see more; they were nearly home and they ran. Their father was standing at the door. 'Where's the woman?' he asked.

'Dunno,' said Jem. 'She sent us out to get wood.'

Then the sound of chewing and swallowing stopped; coming after them was Black Annis, no longer in her cat form. She looked hungry, for her last mouthful had been tough and scrawny. The boys dived into the hut; their father saw the danger, picked up his axe and threw it. It landed in Black Annis' forehead, burying itself deep, and the blood spurted over her face. She stopped; there was nothing she could do now but run back to her cave before she bled to death.

'Jem,' said John, 'did you see? Her blood – it was green.'

'Aye, it was.'

'Will she die now?'

'Don't think so, for she must have a good store of cobweb to stop the bleeding, and besides, I don't think witches do die, but I don't really know.'

'Come,' said their father, 'pull down the skins and let's make a good fire for once.'

Curiously, Black Annis is sometimes associated with a very different female figure: the anchoress Agnes Scott. Agnes Scott was a Dominican nun and chose to live, at least some of her time, in a cave, as a hermit in the woods. She is commemorated on a brass plaque in the church at Swithland. An innocent recluse, given to prayer and pious contemplations and the care of the sick, why should she be in any way associated with the blue-faced child-devouring witch of the Dane Hills? Indeed, what can possibly connect a solitary Dominican nun with the Celtic mother goddess who may sometimes have demanded the odd human sacrifice? Perhaps it is enough just to be solitary, to be odd, to choose to inhabit a cave rather than live close to kith and kin, or be old and have no kin. Or maybe it is sufficient to dress always in long black robes.

THE SHAG DOG

'Have you seen it, Grandma?'

'Don't you dare to question me! There is a dog, and it lives in Shag Dog Pit. No, I've not seen it, but I have heard it: rattling its chain when I've been coming home late at night. They say it comes out of the pit after dark to drink from the River Soar.'

Katie wanted to hear more, but her grandma would only tell her what everyone knew; people going along Black Lane in the dark had been followed by a large mastiff dog, with huge glowing eyes.

'But it never bit them?' Katie pressed.

'No, but I expect they were frightened almost to death!' said Grandpa, closing his eyes again and going back to sleep.

Katie bid her grandparents goodbye, but, as she was leaving, Grandma called out, 'Call in and see how Mrs Whiles is.' The Whileses lived in a big house on Whiles Lane. They had been there so many years that everyone in Birstall knew them.

Tom Whiles was working in the stock yard, putting out straw for the cows, when Katie arrived. 'Have you come to see Mother or me?' he said with a smile, 'or do you want to see the barges being unloaded at the dock?'

He came out through the gate, and Katie took his arm as they walked to the dockside. A barge was tied up there, loaded with Mountsorrel granite, and a small boy stood by the tiller while the horse grazed the canal-side grass.

'Where's the bargee?' Katie asked. 'Surely that young boy can't be in charge?'

'No, the bargee has been down to the White Horse and is already drunk by the looks of him,' said Tom. There, rolling along the towpath, big and tall, came the bargee, wearing a red muffler and yellow waistcoat. When he saw Katie he stopped and a big grin spread across his bearded face. Katie quickly took Tom's arm again, 'Grandma asked me to call and see how your mother is,' she said, as she hurried him away.

They went through the farmyard and into the house, and Katie was shown up to Mrs Whiles' bedroom. There she quickly realised that the old lady was very ill.

'Have you sent for the doctor?' she asked Tom.

'I'll go tonight, after milking.'

'No. That's not good enough!' she said. 'I'll go. Now. I'll get him. Be alright, it's still light, and I'll only be an hour or two. If I go straightaway, I'll be back before it's too dark.'

She walked through the village, past the mill, then down Black Lane, a black cinder path. As she approached Shag Dog Pit she quickened her pace, hurrying, for it was very gloomy and mysterious. The doctor lived in a large house close to Belgrave Church. When she arrived there, she explained to his housekeeper what was wanted, and was told that the doctor would be on his way as soon as he returned home.

Katie now set out for her home as quickly as she could. Her mother would worry if she was out on her own after dark. By the time she reached Black Lane, however, the light was fading fast.

The lane was overhung with trees which made it gloomy and oppressive, but she hurried on. She was halfway along Black Lane when she heard footsteps behind her, and, turning her head, she could just make out the bearded figure of the bargee! He must have waited for her return from Belgrave. To escort her? Or with some other intent?

For the first time in her life, Katie was terrified. She still had at least half a mile to go along Black Lane. If she ran, would he run after her? Would he catch her? She hurried on, then suddenly heard a strange dog's bark. Down the bank from the Shag Dog Pit bounded a large black dog, its jaws open wide and its eyes glowing like burning coals.

It padded behind her on the path, keeping itself between her and the bargee. Katie's heart beat faster. The man's footsteps stopped, and she realised that the dog was protecting her. She rushed forwards and soon saw the light from the blacksmith's home, where she stopped, turned, and looked back. The path was perfectly clear: no dog, and no bargee either.

On the way home, she stopped at the Whileses' house, and told them that the doctor would be along very soon. Tom could see that she had been very frightened, and insisted on knowing what had happened.

The next day Tom went down to the dock, but the barge had gone on its way back to Loughborough, and that bargee was never seen there again.

There are many stories of black dogs; some are witch-creatures, some are ghosts, some are evil, while some, like this one, look after the safety of people who encounter them, protecting them from ill-wishers, as Katie was protected. Another story tells of a wealthy traveller who was accompanied by a black dog while travelling through some woods. The dog vanished as soon as the man rode out of the woods. It was later discovered that two men had been lying in wait for him, but had been discouraged from robbing him by the presence of the dog.

THE WITCH OF EDMONDTHORPE HALL

It was during the time when Oliver Cromwell was the Lord Protector of our green and pleasant land of Leicestershire. Close to Melton Mowbray (now celebrated for its pork pies) there lived, at Edmondthorpe Hall, old Sir Roger Smith, the Lady Ann, and their children.

On the death of his first wife, Sir Roger had travelled to London. There he had been introduced to Ann, the woman who would become his second wife. A dark and very handsome woman, she was said to have come from Aldgate in London, but was actually of Spanish parents, staunch Roman Catholics.

Sir Roger was getting on in years and no longer hunted with the hounds, but Her Ladyship would ride out to see friends in the large family coach with its rampant goat, the family crest, emblazoned on the doors. When the local folk saw her coming, they looked away and hurried back indoors, for they feared the look in her eyes. She seemed to look right through you rather than at you.

The family custom was to spend the Christmas season in London, with their family and friends, which meant that the hall was left in the care of the servants. As Lady Ann was preparing to leave, she spoke to John the butler, reminding him of Cromwell's orders – no merrymaking, singing, dancing, or other traditional Christmas activities.

But, when the cat's away the mice will play, and so it was. No sooner had the family driven away to London than the servants set to, preparing to celebrate Christmas in spite of what the Lord Protector had ruled. They felled a tree to provide the Yule log; then they retrieved the remains of last year's Yule log from the stables and chopped it into kindling with which to light the Christmas fire. The hall was decorated with holly and ivy, and the kitchen staff made the Christmas fare. They feasted, they danced and made merry; they entertained the local mummers on Boxing Day; and so kept Christmas in the good old-fashioned way.

But, by the time the family returned, all was back to normal, and all signs of the merrymaking had been cleared away. Lady Ann alighted from the carriage, entered the house, and stood stock still, rigid in the entrance hall. Turning to John the butler, she demanded to know what had been happening in her absence. John swore that nothing unusual had happened.

'Liar!' she screeched, and proceeded to list the mummers, the singing and dancing, and the name of the fiddler who had played for the dancing! It was as if she had been there in the hall all the time, and knew what food and drink had been consumed. With blazing eyes she turned on John, 'I hold you responsible – you – for any servant that has disobeyed the Lord Protector's rules.'

'How on earth,' thought John, 'could she know so much?' No servant had left the hall to go down to London, and she'd not spoken to anyone else since arriving. John was now a very puzzled and worried man. And he had cause to worry, for Her Ladyship was now more frequently at the hall, paying close attention to the affairs of the kitchen and John's pantry.

By the end of April, John was very unhappy and suffering sleepless nights. One night he sat by his window, thinking about what he should do, when he saw a tired horse coming up the driveway to the hall. He dressed quickly and went out to the stable yard to be met there by the Lady Ann. He helped her to dismount. Without a word, she gave him a withering look and walked past him and into the house. It left him wondering where on earth she'd been at that time of night.

The next day, John was in the kitchen helping the cook to prepare dinner. He was at the chopping block, cutting meat for the pie, when, looking up, he saw a cat crouching on top of a large bread bin: a thin black cat, with cold black eyes. The cat was watching him with a wicked concentration and suddenly sprang at his face. John parried it with the meat chopper that he had in his hand, catching the cat's left paw. The cat screeched and ran limping away, leaving a trail of bloody paw prints behind as it fled into the house.

The cook was the first to react. 'We don't want any strange stray cats in this kitchen, or the house. It will leave blood all over the place if it's not found.'

They looked everywhere, but the cat had completely vanished and was nowhere to be found. While John carried on chopping the meat, the cook set a maid to wash the bloodstains from the flagstones on the kitchen floor. But try as she might, despite the soapy water, sand and rough stone, the stains remained.

That evening, as John stood behind his master's chair, ready to serve dinner, Sir Roger said, 'Your mistress will be a little late this evening. We will wait for her.' Shortly after, she entered, with her left hand bandaged and in a sling. In a flash, John knew exactly what had happened. His mistress was a witch! Lady Ann gave him a cold black-eyed stare and so he held his tongue. What else could he do – Sir Roger would never believe him!

Sir Roger died in 1655 and never did learn the truth about his wife. If you visit the village church at Edmondthorpe you can see his tomb. Sir Roger lies between his two wives. However, from the left wrist of the Lady Ann, and over her long dress, deep in the alabaster, there runs a red stain. To this very day, her wrist is still bleeding.

The hall no longer stands, there being only some romantic ruins left, but, according to the legend, the flagstones in the kitchen had to be changed, for the servants complained that they never could get the floor cleaned of the bloodstains. Then, during the Second World War, the house was requisitioned by the army, but in 1942 it burnt down. The cause of the fire, strange to say, was a black cat, which startled the cook when he was working with a large pan full of hot fat. The pan was overturned, the fat spilt, and the house caught fire and was burned to the ground.

RATS CASTLE

'It's definitely a broomstick sort of night,' thought Tom Tinker on his way to his home near Leicester one evening in late October. The weather was wild and windy, and now there was thunder and lightning, and the intermittent rain in the wind was fast becoming a downpour. 'It's no good,' thought Tom, 'I've got to get out of this rain before me tools and tins get rusty and I get soaked to the skin.'

But where on earth could he shelter? There were no houses or farm buildings handy in the part of the county where he now found himself. In fact, the only place that he thought was close at hand was Rats Castle, and that had a fearful reputation! Folks said that it was haunted, though by whom or what no one was exactly certain. Still, as the thunder grew louder and the rain heavier, Tom decided that beggars couldn't be choosers. He hurried as fast as he could against the wind, and, by the light from the bolts of lightning, he went up the hill and in through the broken door of the castle.

There was a roof on the tower, which meant he was out of the worst of the weather, though rain still came through the slit windows and down the chimney. The upper floor had collapsed, but enough broken floorboards were scattered around to make a fire to warm and dry himself and his belongings. So Tom got cracking and soon had a cosy little fire going in the middle of the floor, as far away from the door, windows and chimney as possible. When he'd got his billycan filled with rainwater, he put it on to boil. A sup of hot tea would be just the thing he thought, and, while he waited for it, he unpacked his tins and tools and carefully laid them out on either side of the fire to dry.

At last the water boiled. He made his tea and poured some into a couple of his tins, settling them into the hot embers at the edge of the fire to keep nice and hot. Then he wrapped his hands around the billycan and took a careful sip, followed by a long slurp, and then sighed gratefully with his eyes closed as it warmed its way down to his stomach. Just at that relaxing moment, there came a sort of coughing grunt from somewhere close by. His eyes flew open and there, across the fire from him, sat the ugliest creature he'd ever seen. Some might have called

it a boggart, some a troll, but Tom, a true lad from Leicester, knew it to be a bogeyman, such as his mother had threatened him with when he was a small and mischievous boy. It was taller than him, and covered in hair. He could see a tail, and horns on its head, and also the most enormous, bulbous nose above a gaping mouth full of fearsome yellow teeth.

'Ey up,' said the bogeyman.

'Er ... hello,' said Tom.

'Aren't yuh frit, then?' said the bogeyman.

'Well, not exackly,' said Tom. 'Have a cuppa tea.' And at that, Tom grabbed his pincers and picked up a very hot tin full of tea from the edge of the fire and handed it across to the bogeyman.

Well, the bogeyman took hold of that nearly red-hot tin and tossed the tea down his throat. Then he crumpled that tin up into a ball and threw it directly back at Tom Tinker. It was a jolly good job that Tom had played a lot of tip and run, because, quick as a flash, he upped with the pincers and smashed that tin ball straight back at the bogeyman. It hit him full in the mouth, and out flew a couple of very large teeth, so that he gave a terrible howl, clapped his hands to his mouth, and then jumped up and fled through the door into the rain.

'Well,' thought Tom, as he looked ruefully at his rather battered pincers, 'I'm glad he's gone – perhaps I can get back to my tea again.'

But no sooner had he blissfully slurped some more tea, than he heard a very loud coughing grunt again. Another bogeyman! And if the first one was ugly, this one was twice as ugly, twice the size, and with two heads into the bargain.

'Err ... helll-o,' said Tom.

'Aren't yuh frit, then?' said the bogeyman.

'Err ... not exackly,' answered Tom. 'Have a cuppa tea.'

Again Tom grabbed his pincers and took the other red-hot tin out from the edge of the fire and handed it across to the bogeyman. But, remembering what had happened last time, he dropped the pincers and picked up his soldering iron. The bogeyman tossed half the tea into one mouth and the rest into the other. So Tom was ready this time when the bogeyman scrunched the tin up into a ball and threw it back to him. He gave it a good clout with the soldering iron and hit the bogeyman in one mouth; it bounced off and straight into the other mouth as the two heads turned towards each other. Six-inch teeth flew through the air, and his howls were twice as loud as the first's as he fled and squeezed himself out through the door.

Tom began to wonder what on earth was going to happen next. As he finished off his tea, he soon found out. There came some strange scrabbling noises from the chimney, and then a large hand appeared and began feeling around the floor. Quickly, Tom picked up a large hammer and brought it down hard upon that groping hand. A loud howl came echoing down the chimney as the hand was swiftly withdrawn. Tom decided that it was probably not safe to stay there any longer, for fear of something worse.

'I don't care if it is still raining, I'm off!'

With that said, he began putting all his tins back in their sack, and all his tools away in his bag, except for his hammer, which he kept handy just in case! He then picked up his tool-bag and the sack, and, slinging them over his shoulders, made his way towards the door. He was nearly there, when a terrible creaking and groaning came from up above him, and to his horror he saw that two huge hands were lifting up the roof on one side of the tower. There then appeared not one ghastly head, not even two heads, but three of them all on one set of shoulders, and each head terrible to behold.

'Ey up down there,' they chorused.

'Err … err … hello,' quavered Tom.

'Aren't yuh frit, then?' they bellowed.

'N-not exackly,' shouted Tom, trying to keep his courage up. 'I'm sorry, you're too late for some tea; but if you'll wait a bit, I'll just pop home for me sledgehammer!'

With that, he hurried out of the door and promptly tripped over a very large tail. So, pulling some nails out of his pocket, he quickly nailed the end of the tail to the remains of the door to encourage the bogeyman to wait. He then scurried off through the rain as fast as he could go, and didn't stop until he reached home. Whether or not the bogeyman waited for his return, Tom Tinker never knew, because, of course, he never, ever, went back to Rats Castle.

Note:

I've never discovered the exact whereabouts of Rats Castle – where it is, or was, supposed to be; though I can perhaps make some guesses. The Romans called the fort and settlement that they made at Leicester *Ratae Coritanorum* (or *Corieltauvorum*), after the fort of the Coritani (or Corieltavi) tribe. This was on the actual site of the Roman fort, but there was also a rath or hill fort nearby at a village now called Ratby. The Normans built themselves a motte-and-bailey castle on the site of the Romans' fort, and memories of all these settlements could have combined to create the setting for this tale. It could, however, have the more boring explanation of being a ruined old inn left to the tender mercies of hordes of rats – which could, of course, be anywhere in the county.

BEL THE GIANT

(This story was originally told to me by a Mrs Frank in 1947, when I was just a lad.)

It had been a long hot day in the fields and the giant Bel and his men had retired to the local alehouse to quench their thirst and meet their friends. By the time their jars had been emptied a few times tongues began to wag, and Bel, being a great horse lover and a gambling man, made a bet that the horse he had just bought could jump from the top of their local hill into Leicester, the nearby town, in just one leap.

'No,' said all his friends. 'No way.'

So when the debates had finished, the bet was agreed at 'three jumps between the hill and Leicester town'. Wagers were placed in the hands of the landlord and early next morning Bel and his friends met at Bel's stables. Bel saddled and readied his new sorrel mare. His friends meanwhile had collected their horses and saddled up ready to ride down the road towards the town.

Having given them a good head start, Bel mounted his horse and rode off up the local hill. As he reached the top, the horse broke into a gallop and then she took a mighty leap. She cleared a mill on the River Soar, landing some distance further on. She jumped again, landing very hard, and broke the saddle girths. A third time she leapt, a great and mighty leap; she landed and stumbled, throwing Bel to the ground, where he lay stunned. Exhausted now, the dying mare staggered and fell, crushing that mighty man, the giant Bel. So it was that upon that day, horse and rider they died together.

His friends, finding Bel and his horse both dead on the ground, decided to bury him on the spot where he had fallen. That evening in the alehouse, they drank deep to the memory of their best friend, and all agreed that though he had not reached Leicester town, it was a great feat that should be remembered. So the places where he had landed were renamed. Mount Sorrel, where his sorrel mare was mounted; One Leap, where she first landed; Burst All, where the saddle girths broke; and Bel's Grave, where they buried him, about half a mile from where I was born.

> Mountsorrel he was mounted at,
> Rothley he rode by,
> Wanlip he leaped over,
> Birstall he burst his gall,
> And Belgrave he was buried at.

> Mountsorrel is a stony place,
> Sileby it be sandy,
> Rothley has the halfway house,
> Quorndon is the dandy.

5

GUILDHALL
ENTERTAINERS

Borough records show that as many as fifty-six companies of travelling actors performed here in Leicester during the late sixteenth century. Though we do not know for sure whether Shakespeare himself ever visited the Guildhall, the actors of the Earl of Leicester's company are known to have played here. There are some ancient hooks high up on the ceiling beams in the Great Hall which are thought to have been used to hang the stage curtains or the scenery cloths. We are not sure exactly which plays the Earl of Leicester's men gave at the Guildhall, but it is tempting to imagine that the players would have known something of the stories pertaining to Leicester's past and chosen accordingly. We do know that Shakespeare's friend and fellow actor Richard Burbage was with the company when it came to the Guildhall, and Burbage was famous for his portrayal of two of Shakespeare's kingly characters, Lear and Richard III. However, we do not know whether Burbage gave either his Lear or his Richard to the audience here. Both of these characters have connections to the old town of Leicester. Shakespeare's stories, though, differ slightly from the following tales.

KING LEIR

Long, long ago, long before the Romans came to this land, there was a Celtic kingdom ruled by King Bladud. Said by Geoffrey of Monmouth to be a descendant of Aeneas, Bladud was a learned magician, believed to possess the power of flight (he died in a particularly nasty flying accident). Bladud was succeeded by his son Leir, who ruled his kingdom well for a great many years. Early in his reign, Leir established his court on land by the River Soar. He named the place Caerleir, though in later years the Saxons were to call it Leircester.

King Leir was never blessed with any sons, though he had three daughters – Goneril, Regan and Cordelia – and while he loved all of his daughters, the youngest, Cordelia, was his favourite. Now, as he grew older and frailer, Leir began to find ruling the kingdom increasingly tiring, and so he decided it was time to share some of the burden, and prepare for the time when his reign would end. He therefore resolved to divide the kingdom between his three daughters. He would marry them to worthy husbands who would help them rule. However, he foolishly decided that the largest and richest part of his kingdom was to go to whichever daughter he judged loved him best: 'To her that loves most, most shall be given.'

> So on a time it pleased the King
> A question thus to move
> Which of his daughters to his grace
> Could show the dearest love,
> For to my age you bring content
> Quoth he, then let me hear

Which of you three in plighted troth
The kindest will appear.

A hush fell on the gathered court as Goneril stood and curtsied to the King, her father. 'Father, dearer to me than the light of the sun, than the sweetness of fine wine or the bite of good bread, dearer thou art to me than mine own soul,' she began:

And for your sake my bleeding heart
Shall here be cut in twain
Ere I see your reverend grace
The smallest grief sustain

Well, this delighted her father, and he pronounced that she should have a third of the kingdom, and a say in whom she would marry.

Next, Regan made her way through the crowded hall to the dais where the King sat. 'Dear father, dearer than all others, more dear than child or husband can be to me,' she said, flinging herself to her knees:

For your sake
The worst of all extremities
I'll gently undertake
And serve your Highness night and day
With diligence and love
That sweet content and quietness
Discomforts may remove.

(She was not going to be outdone by her sister in her effort to get the best from her father.)

Proud and happy to hear these declarations of love for him, Leir promised Regan the same as he had promised Goneril.

Finally, he turned to his favourite daughter, Cordelia. 'Daughter, you my youngest, now tell me how great is the love you bear for me? Speak. Let all those gathered here at this court know of your love for me, your father.'

Now, Cordelia was shocked by the false protestations of her older sisters, their insincerity. She stood, silent and stunned, the firelight gleaming on the gold around her neck.

'Father, could any daughter honestly claim to love her father more than as a father? I have always loved you as my father, and will always do so. Know this: as you have worth, whatever you possess, so I love you for who you are, my father,' she said:

> The love
> Which to your Grace I owe
> Shall be the duty of the child.
> And that is all I'll show.

Her father, comparing her words with the extravagant speeches of her sisters, was greatly disappointed, hurt and angry. 'As you cannot love me as your sisters do,' he roared, 'you shall have no part of this, my kingdom. Henceforth I banish thee from my court. Thou art no child of mine.' Leir's eyes bulged, and his face grew white with anger as he looked first at his daughter then at the assembled court. 'This that was my child, I cast her off. Let it be known that here I give her as wife to any man that would take her. Give her in marriage, but a marriage with no dowry.' Leir flung his cloak about his shoulders and stomped out the great chamber.

So King Leir sought husbands for his two elder daughters. Goneril was married to Maglaunus, Duke of Albany, and

Regan to Henvin, Duke of Cornwall. Leir then divided the kingdom in two. One half he retained, while the other was divided between Goneril and Regan. They would receive the second part of their inheritance when he died.

Then Leir turned his thoughts to Cordelia. Aganippus, King of the Franks (hearing of Cordelia's beauty and knowing her story) had asked for her hand in marriage. He had fallen so much in love with her that he wished to marry her despite King Leir's refusal to settle any dowry upon her. So it was that Cordelia was married. She then left her dearly loved father and her native land, and went to Gaul with Aganippus where 'she gentler fortunes found'. Though King Leir was old, he remained in good health for many years and showed no sign of preparing to die. This was increasingly looked on with disfavour by the two dukes and the daughters that they had married. Finally they grew tired of waiting to inherit the rest of the kingdom. They rebelled, stripped Leir of the crown, and took the rest of the kingdom from him.

After much debate and negotiation, Duke Maglaunus finally agreed to house King Leir with a retinue of sixty knights, servants and his bard, at the court in Albany. For a while all went well for Leir, but after two years Goneril had grown fed up with her father. She became increasingly irritated and angry with his quarrelsome and volatile retinue. She and her servants started to treat them casually, disrespectfully, and eventually the knights objected and rebelled against this treatment. Goneril then demanded that, as his retinue was so troublesome to her, her father should get rid of at least half of them.

King Leir was incensed by this treatment and immediately left the court of the Duke of Albany, with his sixty knights, servants and his faithful bard, and travelled the length of the island of Britain, to the court of the Duke of Cornwall. There he was received with honour. Unfortunately this did not last, as, within the year, there were arguments, fights and drunken brawls between the two households, and Leir was ordered by Regan to get rid of his retinue, save only five. This was an insult too much to bear.

He returned to Goneril, hoping that she would have pity on him. At least she had only told him to get rid of half his followers. He was sadly disappointed. She was as angry and as determined to reduce his household as she had ever been.

'Why do you need all these servants, these knights? Can you afford to keep them yourself? If you cannot afford them, then why should you expect me to? You can stay here only if you dismiss them all, save just the one knight to serve you!'

King Leir now realised that neither of these daughters were going to support his retinue. He had given his kingdom and all his wealth to them, and could no longer support his knights himself. Sadly, he was forced to keep the service of only one knight and dismiss all the rest. But this was unbearable. He began to think of trying his luck with his youngest daughter, Cordelia – though he was uncertain what his reception would be, for Leir now remembered how badly he had treated her.

But his life was now so miserable. This once-proud king – this wealthy, powerful, leader of a much-feared war band – was now an outcast and a beggar. It could not be any worse. The aged Leir was beginning to understand the truth of Cordelia's words. Unlike her sisters, she actually loved him for himself, not for his possessions.

So King Leir set out for Gaul. In abject poverty, having been forced to beg for both food and shelter on his journey, he finally arrived in Gaul, at the gates of the settlement where

his daughter and her husband, the King Aganippus, held court. He sent his knight with a message to her. Humbly, he begged for her forgiveness and for her compassion.

When Cordelia heard of his condition, she was moved to tears. She would restore to him his dignity, then welcome him to her court. The messenger was sent with money and told, 'See that he is bathed, clothed and fed. Find accommodation for him and treat him as an invalid until he is restored to health and wellbeing. Provide him with whatever else he needs and engage a retinue, knights, servants, and bards to do him honour, sing his praise and recount his victories. When he is recovered, escort him back here. Here he will be received with honour and joy by his loving daughter.'

And so it was done, just as she desired. King Leir was welcomed by King Aganippus and happily reunited with his youngest daughter, Queen Cordelia. Having heard of the vile, dishonourable treatment accorded to Leir, they then raised a mighty army. This army set sail across the sea to Britain. There, the King of the Franks and his Queen fought those two greedy sons-in-law and their wives, defeated them, took their land and cast them out.

King Leir regained his kingdom. He ruled the realm until, some three years later, he died. Cordelia then became Queen of Britain. Her first act was to arrange the burial of her father. She had an underground chamber constructed beneath the River Soar at Caerleir, and there King Leir was laid to rest.

Today, if you walk along the River Soar to the north of the city of Leicester, you will find yourself in Watermead Park. There, between the river and the Grand Union Canal, you will find a series of flooded gravel pits, one of which is named King Lear's Lake in memory of that ancient king who founded the city.

So on a time it pleased the King,
A question thus to move,
Which of his daughters to his grace,
Could show the dearest love,
For to my age you bring content,
Quoth he, then let me hear,
Which of you three in plighted troth,
The kindest will appear.

(*A Book of Old English Ballads*)

THE KING'S BED

Leicester has acquired an unfortunate reputation, for an old legend states that it is unlucky for the reigning sovereign to pay a visit to this town. Henry III, with his young son and heir Edward, visited Leicester, and very soon afterwards the King and his family were taken prisoner by the barons and Simon de Montfort. In 1390 Richard II came to Leicester Castle, and sometime after that met a very sad and sticky end. As a young girl, and long before her nine days as Queen, Lady Jane Grey visited the town of Leicester on her way to join the household of Catherine Parr. She was presented with a gallon of wine by the good burghers of Leicester. (This was no compensation for any subsequent beheading.) And we should not forget the much-detested sovereign Lord King Charles, the first of that name. Accompanied by his Queen, Charles paid the town the honour of a visit. Alas, poor deluded monarch.

But good Queen Bess, Elizabeth I, she never came here, though visits had been talked of and planned, and preparations made. Were there wise and discerning soothsayers among her courtiers? Was she warned in some way to avoid the town? And as for Richard III, well, he had obviously never heard the legend, and anyway, he would have had far more important matters to cogitate upon.

Richard III arrived in Leicester on 20 August 1485, bringing with him his own special bed, for the King slept badly in strange beds. The royal bed was erected in the very best chamber in the White Boar inn. No doubt the innkeeper was delighted to accommodate the royal visitor, for the sign

over his inn was most appropriate. It was the sign of a white boar, and the white boar was the device emblazoned upon King Richard's royal standard.

The King had a good night's sleep and left early the next day to confront the rebel forces of Henry Tudor at Bosworth Field. As he rode out of Leicester and onto Bow Bridge, his heel caught against one of the cornerstones. A local wise woman is reputed to have said:

> Mark where his armed heel
> Strikes against the bridge,
> His head shall crack,
> But he'll not feel it.
> He'll ride alone,
> As cold as stone,
> Crookback.

What happened at the Battle at Bosworth is pretty well recorded. But what happened afterwards? The story goes that as

Richard's body was borne back to Leicester, his head struck the very cornerstone predicted by the wise woman.

Richard's corpse was placed in a common stone coffin and displayed for two days in the collegiate church, before being buried in the chapel of Greyfriars Friary. Some ten years later, King Henry VII had an alabaster tombstone erected over the grave. It cost him £10 1*d*. This tombstone, however, was destroyed at the time of the Dissolution of the Monasteries, and King Richard's stone coffin – minus his body – could then be found serving as a horse trough in the yard of the White Horse inn in Gallowtree Gate.

What may not be so well known is what happened to the royal bed, left at the inn when Richard set off to his last battle at Bosworth Field. First, as news of the defeat of the King's forces was carried back to Leicester, the innkeeper hurriedly changed the name of his inn from the White Boar to the Blue Boar. This was a prudent measure, the blue boar being the insignia on the banners borne by the Earl of Richmond's forces (Richmond was an important supporter of Henry Tudor). Someone must have got busy with the paintbrush very hastily.

As for the bed, well, it was safer not to advertise its existence too widely, so it stayed largely ignored for some years. This emblematic piece of royal furniture remained in the inn, passed down from landlord to landlord with other 'fixtures and fittings', until the early 1600s. At that time, mistress Agnes Clarke, wife to the landlord, needed to move the ancient bed. To her astonishment, as she shifted it, a gold coin fell to the floor and rolled under her foot. Excited and impatient, Agnes found some tools and set about dismantling the bed. She found it to have a false base and, hidden in this base, she found treasure – £300. Coins, some from the reign of Richard III and

some from even earlier times, spilled onto the floor. This was a lot of money at the time – a king's ransom, you might say.

It was an immense fortune to Agnes and her husband Thomas, and they were determined that it should remain theirs and stay secret. It is, however, hard not to indulge in a little unaccustomed luxury, some small extra spending – a costly new coat, shoes from the most expensive shoemaker in town. Small extravagances, but noticeable to sharp-eyed neighbours. Tongues began to wag: 'What could be the source of this wealth? The secret of the humble innkeepers' new-found good fortune?' Even after her husband's death, when Agnes herself had become the landlady of the Blue Boar, she was still attracting attention. 'How does the landlady, the widow, maintain such style?'

It was not long before a young woman, one Alice Grumbold, applied for work at the inn and was taken on as maid to Agnes.

She worked hard, at the same time keeping a very sharp eye on her mistress, and soon she had uncovered some of the secrets of the wealth hidden in the inn.

Then Alice began to plan and plot with a group of her acquaintances, and one evening seven men booked themselves into the Blue Boar as travellers needing shelter for the night. Darkness fell, and when all was quiet the thieves began to load their horses with any valuables that they could find about the inn. However, something must have disturbed Agnes, for she woke, and, discovering what was afoot, began to scream for help. Alice, in an effort to keep the landlady quiet, stuffed two fingers down the screaming woman's throat. This silenced the unfortunate Agnes; it choked her to death.

The thieves were very soon apprehended, imprisoned and tried. Alice Grumbold was burnt at the stake and the seven men were hanged.

The Blue Boar was pulled down in 1836, and no one knows for certain what happened to the bed which had hidden such wealth, and in which King Richard III spent the night before battle, the last night of his life.

6

UNFORTUNATE MAIDENS

Leicestershire and Rutland are counties of gentle hills, valleys and woodlands, studded with quiet but prosperous villages. Over time many great houses have been built among these hills and valleys, situated mostly at a little distance from the nearby villages. Surrounded by great swathes of forest and parkland, they were established for the rich and powerful of the land. But, however mighty or famous, however noble, their owners may once have been, some of these fabulous houses have since fallen victim to neglect and decay. Some have completely disappeared; some lie ruined and abandoned, guarding the stories of their rich histories. So, what more suitable setting for the sad stories of unhappy maidens than these once-magnificent, now decaying, mansions, built in times long past?

THE SILVER SLIPPERS

In the early years of the eighteenth century a woman crouched beside a meagre fire, seeking warmth from its flames. It was a late autumn afternoon and the attic room in which she sat

was cramped and barely lit. It allowed just space enough for a
narrow bed and a small wooden chest. Above the bed, a grimy
window let in the dying light of day. The woman listened and
waited, holding thin hands to the fire, and bit her lip as she
heard footsteps. Slowly they ascended the long flight of stairs.
She heard the rasp of a key in the lock and the door opened.
Just inside the room, a hand placed a half loaf of dark bread,
a small jug filled with water, and some sticks for the fire. An
empty jug was removed and once more the door was locked.

Painfully she made her way to the door, grasped the jug and
drank, then took the wood and fed the fire. She left the bread
on the floor and stumbled to the bed, pulling the coverings
over her. As she lay under the soiled and threadbare blankets,
light from the fire fell on her face, showing it to be pinched
and grey with pain. But this was no broken old woman.
Though cold, ill, and in despair, the prisoner in the attic of
Papillon Hall was young and strangely beautiful. She was also
a stranger, a foreigner, in this rural corner of Leicestershire.
She understood little English and spoke less. She lay shivering
with fever, watching the room grow dark. Far below she could
hear voices, men's harsh laughter; in the fine rooms of the hall,
David Papillon – or Young Pamp as he was known locally –
was entertaining. The neighbouring gentry were gathered to

celebrate his forthcoming nuptials. The drink circulated and the talk flowed, interrupted by snatches of song and drunken oaths. The following day the new Lord Papillon would ride to London to marry the woman his late father had chosen for him.

Unsteadily he rose to his feet, swayed, and waved a half-empty bottle of brandy above his head. 'Friends, err gentlemen, a toast to me and my damn bride. And one to my father, curse the fellow.'

'Aye, fathers, always interfering, don't leave well alone.'

'Too old they be, old and umm bothersome, yes, very bothering of us, well, what I means is of their sons, their own flesh and blood.'

All those gathered that evening at Papillon Hall knew of the terms of the will, knew that Young Pamp would be disinherited should he choose not to marry the woman selected for him by his late father.

David Papillon drained the bottle of brandy, stumbled across the room to the large window and looked out into the night. Suddenly he staggered, his head heavy; he fell against the long table and lay down amongst the jumble of bottles, glasses and spilt drinks, and felt hot tears run down his cheeks. And the young lord remembered the girl in the attic, her heartbreakingly lovely face, her green eyes, her tumbling dark hair. He could still feel how frail she had seemed, how delicate in his arms. And how she had struggled. Struggled, screamed, resisted him. Yes, she had resisted him at first.

In his mind's eye he saw again the modest hostelry on the road to Madrid, saw her father the innkeeper, watched the old man as, furtively, he accepted the offered bribe and pocketed the golden sovereigns. He remembered how the father had turned his back on his daughter, turned a blind eye to her seduction, allowed the lord to carry off his child. Remembered too her desperate pleading to be let go. And he recalled how long it had been before she calmed. Before she gave in to him. Before she could no longer refuse his declarations of undying love, his solemn promise that when they reached England he would make her his legally married wife.

As Young Pamp lay slumped across the table, dreaming of the woman he had so wronged, his guests emptied the decanters, drank the dregs from the brandy bottles, called for horses and departed. The heavy doors to the hall banged shut and the clatter of hooves drifted in through the window of the attic room where the woman lay. She was cold, so cold. It would be daylight before Jeremy climbed the stairs, unlocked the door and relit the fire. Twice each day he brought her a bowl of soup, tended the fire and left. He never spoke.

Jeremy Buckman, known as Jez Coach, was head coachman at Papillon Hall. It was he who had driven his young master across Europe on the grand tour. And it was he who had whipped up the horses as Young Pamp carried off his prize, his victim. Back home in Gumley, Jez said nothing of the woman in the attic. It was not his place to speak of what had happened. And he had been well paid.

As dawn broke, Lord Papillon mounted his favourite mare and rode off to London and wedlock. The woman in the attic room drifted in and out of an uneasy sleep. She was dreaming of that time when she had first begun to fall under the spell of the handsome English lord, had believed him when, in broken Spanish, he had vowed that he meant to marry her. Slowly she had allowed herself to trust him. She had imagined marriage, comfort, even riches. A loving husband and, perhaps, children. In her dream she lived again that time when she had dared to enjoy some happiness, the few days in Paris when he had bought her clothes and silver brocade slippers. Slippers which had fitted so perfectly, and kept her feet ready to dance.

She gasped and woke, feeling a tightening in her chest. She struggled to take breath and clutched at her side as pains engulfed her, till she found a shallow breath, opened her eyes and lay still. In the dim light of early dawn she could just make out the walls of the room, the fireplace, and the wooden chest in which there was a skirt, an old patched shawl and the silver slippers. With the slippers was the bill for their purchase.

Fully awake now, she lay thinking of her first days in Leicestershire, when he had been so kind, so loving, to her. She had worn the slippers and they had danced together through the silent rooms of the hall. But then the messenger had arrived. His father was dead. Killed in London after falling from his horse. The will was read and she had seen his face. The confusion written there; the horror, the anger. Then she had been hidden away in the attic of Papillon Hall and assured that it would not be for long – just a few days until it was all sorted out.

But how long had she been shut away? Days? Weeks? She no longer knew. All she knew was the pain in her chest, in her heart, and how hard it was to breathe. Struggling for air, she cursed her pain, her weakness. Cursed him, cursed her father, cursed herself for believing him and allowing herself to trust, cursed the days of false happiness and the time when she had danced for joy.

The woman reached her hand from under the covers, felt for the chest and took out the slippers. Tucked into the toe of the left slipper was the bill of purchase. She studied the crumpled paper, knowing that she must write a plea … a curse … her story ... an accusation. She climbed from the bed, crawled to the empty fireplace and licked her finger. Then she rubbed the moistened finger in the soot and wrote smeared, barely legible, words on the back of the torn bill of purchase. She folded the paper and tucked it away in the toe of an elegant and extremely expensive silver brocade slipper. As she put the slippers back in the chest, the woman felt a sharp, unbearable pain.

Later that day, Jez Coach climbed the stairs to the locked room, found the uneaten bread, and saw her lying face-down on the floor. He turned her body over and closed her eyes, then crossed himself and stood looking at the dead woman.

'Well lass, here's a to-do. Though mayhap master'll not grieve overmuch ... not today that's for sure, not whiles him's in London doing his marrying. Happen new wife will bring him some luck, not like you lass, with that pretty face on you. Told him I did, said no good would come of it, yous being a Spanish lass. Well now what's to be doing with you? Can't be burying you for you're not here ... isn't nobody here but me and Rosie the cook, that's official, and given out to all the neighbourhood by master himself. Shut the door ... forget you ... better wait till master'll say what's to be done.'

Jez Coach pushed the body under the bed, picked up the water jug and the bowl, and locked the door of the attic room behind him.

Weeks passed, months, years before the door was unlocked and the room opened.

Young Pamp was far too busy enjoying his new wife's money to bother with a rather rundown country house in Leicestershire. Although no beauty, his bride was by no means ugly, and, some years older than him, she was considerably more sophisticated than her 'country yokel' bridegroom.

The newly-weds began their marriage by redecorating her London residence; there were furnishings to be acquired, curtains and wall hangings to be chosen, chandeliers to be bought for the great rooms, and paintings to be commissioned. And there was the theatre and the opera to attend, the racing to follow, and gaming houses to frequent. Thus, the new Lord Papillon managed the first years of his marriage in reasonable comfort; he seldom saw his wife, save when she presided at the tea table. A marriage of inconvenience lacking all mutual understanding, it lasted until she died some six years later.

Only then, a newly bereaved widower, did David Papillon return to his country seat. A butler, two housemaids and a scullery maid were engaged. Rosie the cook was long dead so a woman from nearby was employed, while a lad came daily to help old Jez the coachman. After years of neglect, Papillon Hall was coming back to life. One morning Jenny, the second housemaid, was cleaning down the attic stairs when, in one dusty corner, she spotted a key – the key to the door of the long-closed room. Curious, she unlocked the door and went in, saw the wooden chest and took out an old skirt. Under the skirt she found a pair of silver brocade slippers. Hardly daring to touch them, so beautiful were they, she took them to the butler, who handed them to his master.

Then, for the first time, Old Pamp felt stirrings of guilt. As he studied the elegant little slippers, her presence seemed to fill the room; he could hear her soft Spanish lisp, and he remembered how the shoemaker had measured her feet, remembered her delight in their silvery sheen. Remembered also the time after – his cruelty, his greed, his cowardly choices. And guilt became his companion. Terrible, ever-present, remorse and self-contempt.

These feelings of shame might, in another man, have engendered some sympathy for his servants, his tenants, his neighbours or the tradesmen of the area. In Old Pamp self-hatred grew into dislike of his fellow man. Lonely, angry and guilt-ridden he became ever more surly and selfish. He was feared, avoided and hated, and when he fell while out with the hounds and was killed, none mourned.

Papillon Hall passed to a cousin with a large family of daughters. Once more the hall was alive with young voices and laughter. There was entertainment, dances, parties. One day the eldest girl was rummaging through a chest in the room which had been Old Pamp's bedchamber, when she came across the slippers and slipped them on her feet. They fitted, but there was something in the right slipper. She examined the bill of purchase but could make nothing of it, so took it to her father. He realised that the language was Spanish and, with a certain amount of difficulty, managed to decipher the words which had been spelled out, all those years before, in soot from the fireplace. He read: 'Remember me – these slippers. Curse him that removes them.'

'So we have a curse and a beautiful pair of slippers. Where to put them? In the library perhaps, on a shelf high enough to see but not to move?' he said to his very excited daughters.

Years passed and new owners came to the hall. The curse was forgotten until, in 1866, the slippers were removed to Leicester. Strange and frightening noises began to be heard at night, so they were hastily returned. The noises stopped.

The hall was sold again, to a Mr Holford, who sent the slippers to an exhibition in Paris, and life at the hall became so uncomfortable that, once again, they were returned and, in 1884, they were locked into a special glass case for safety.

In the first years of the twentieth century a new owner, Captain Belville, decided to make alterations to the building. He sent the slippers to his solicitor's office for safekeeping. There were dire consequences; one of the men engaged on the renovations was killed by falling bricks, and other workmen suffered minor injuries. The slippers were returned. It was during this work on the hall that the Captain discovered the skeleton in the attic. No record of her death could be found, nor indeed of her life. Who was she? None could tell. Had there been a murder? When had she died? Where was she from?

Stories circulated of times long past, of locked rooms, of past owners, of Old Pamp, hated and feared. And tales were told of curses and of slippers. Captain Belville, however, seems to have ignored these stories, for once again he sent the slippers away. This time he allowed them to be exhibited in the museum at Leicester. While they were on show in the museum, not only did he have a bad fall from his horse, but also a tremendous thunderstorm set fire to the hall, killing three of his horses. Two men working around the building are also believed to have died in the storm. The slippers were brought back to the hall and locked away. Then Captain Belville flung the key into the pond.

During the Second World War, officers of the 82nd Airborne Division were billeted at the hall. When on two occasions the slippers were removed, those responsible were reported killed or missing. When the war ended and Papillon Hall was abandoned, only one slipper could be found – and it was not until the hall was finally demolished in 1951 that the second one was discovered under a floorboard.

The silver brocade slippers were finally given into the charge of Leicester Arts & Museums Services, and it seems that the curse may at last have been worked out.

RED COMYN

All around, the storm growled. Clouds were gathering, hovering over her. As she cowered in the hollow oak, Lady Agnes Ferrars couldn't believe how such a bright and promising May Day had turned into this nightmare. Like a hunted deer, she was aware of the sounds of pursuit, sometimes closing in and sometimes fading into the distance. She knew that this hollow tree could only provide her with temporary shelter. Her pursuers would not give up. They didn't dare give up, for they were as afraid of the anger of Lord Comyn as she. Lady Agnes' only hope was to reach the Priory of Grace Dieu, but that would involve travelling over a rough, unknown landscape in increasingly menacing weather.

Life at Groby Hall had been pleasant and uneventful for Lady Agnes Ferrars, the only child of Lord Ferrars. At seventeen she was of an age to marry and she knew that her standing as heir to the family fortune would bring her plenty of suitors to choose from. Fortunately for Agnes, Lord Ferrars was a loving and doting father, who – unusually in the fourteenth century – cared more for his daughter's happiness than for adding to his lands or wealth. He would allow Agnes to choose her own husband, within reason. He was not really worried that Agnes would choose anyone he considered unsuitable, for she had always been a loving and considerate daughter, giving her parents little to worry about.

Then one autumn everything changed. King Edward had been involved in a fierce and bloody war against the Scots. Some of the Scottish clan chiefs had joined with Edward against their own king. One such was 'Red' Comyn, so called because of his flaming red hair and his flaming red temper. He was courageous, foolhardy in battle, and driven by hatred of the Bruce. Comyn believed himself to have the stronger claim to the Scottish crown.

As a reward, and to keep him loyal, Edward had granted Comyn Whitwick Castle and the lands around it, which were rich in forest and game for hunting. Red Comyn was a giant of a man, with height and strength and immense appetites, and he and his men spent most of their time hunting across his land and in the forest around. His men were really his own private army, owing their lives and therefore their loyalty to their lord. This marauding band of hunters thought nothing of riding over other people's land and into other forests. His neighbours found it unwise to complain as Red Comyn's revenge was swift and vicious and, as he was favoured by the King, there was nothing anyone could do. He and his men were often in fights with the locals, mostly peasants and yeomen, no match for Comyn's ferocious band of fighters.

Comyn's other pastimes were drinking and enjoying any young women he came across. No young girl was safe if she caught his eye. Red Comyn believed that whatever or whoever he wanted, he had the right to have. He acted, and taught his men to act, without heart or conscience.

By the spring Comyn was bored. He had hunted so much that most of the game on his own estate was dead. He felt he needed more land and it was then that Lady Agnes Ferrars came to his attention. What more could he ask for? She was young and beautiful, with skin like a peach, hair that shone like spun gold, eyes as innocent and blue as a periwinkle and, most importantly, she was heiress to lands and wealth that surpassed his own. Red Comyn wanted her and was determined that he would have her.

However, Lady Agnes was not the daughter of a poor peasant or an ignorant yeoman. She was the daughter of nobility. This time the King would not turn a blind eye if Comyn took her by force. He decided he must win her by stealth. He wooed her. He sent flowers. He sent messages. He even sent her a minstrel to sing to her, then had the man killed when the music got him nowhere with the lady. He made sure to appear at any gatherings of local gentry where she might be. He dressed in his finest clothes to appear presentable and kept himself in check enough to be courteous. While in her presence he refrained from too much drink. However, when he was near her he could see that she regarded him with disdain. Never did she warm to him, and her father made no effort to hide his horror at Lord Comyn's approaches. Red Comyn was not a man of patience. He needed another plan.

By the end of April, Agnes and her father were convinced that Lord Comyn had lost interest in her. They had not seen him or received anything from him for some weeks. What they did not realise was that the Scottish lord had set some of his men to watch the hall in secret and report back to him if anything should happen that might be to his advantage.

The day dawned bright and fair on 1 May. It was the feast day of St Philip and St James. The Ferrars family and their household were to go to the church in Ratby to celebrate there. Unfortunately, just before they were due to leave, Lady Agnes' favourite mare was found to be too lame to ride. She persuaded her parents that she would only worry about her horse if she went to the celebrations and so she would stay behind. After much discussion it was decided that Nan, her elderly nurse, would stay with her in case she needed anything.

Agnes sat in the tall window above the main door of the hall, watching as the party prepared to set off for Ratby Church. Among the riders she could see her father. She noticed he was mounted on the new bay mare rather than his favourite, the enormous and hard-to-handle stallion called Hector. The riders set off and, as they rode out of sight, he turned and gestured a farewell salute to his daughter.

Now all was quiet; outside, the stable boy shovelled up some piles of dung and then retreated round the hall to the stables at the back. The servants who had not gone to church were busy in the kitchens, and the only sound in her chamber was the irritated tutting of old Nan, her nurse, as she found another line of false stitching in her embroidery.

Agnes wished she could be out riding on such a beautiful day, but Blossom would not be fit for some days yet. She stood up and stretched. She would go to the stables to see how her horse was, taking some apples to feed both Blossom and Hector. 'Come, Nan, let's take these to the stables,' she said, reaching for the dish of apples that stood on the table. Old Nan put down her embroidery and hurried to keep up. Brought up on a farm with lots of younger siblings, she was much more at home with horses and children than with needles and thread.

They pushed open the heavy double doors to the stable. Inside it was dark; they could just make out the horses and the stable boy sweeping out some of the empty stalls. Agnes went in to Hector's stall. He was big, and restless after being cooped up, yet he quietened under her hand and took the offered apple. Then she went to see Blossom. The mare was nervous and rolled her eyes anxiously as the girl inspected the damaged foreleg. Agnes had some difficulty calming the mare, and stood feeding her and quietly stroking her for some time.

Suddenly there was the sound of hooves on the cobbles in the yard outside. Agnes ran to the door, opening it just a crack, and peered out. What she saw made her blood run cold. In the stable yard were two of Red Comyn's men. She knew there would be others at the door of the hall itself. She saw them dismount.

Old Nan pushed her into a dark corner, flinging an old horse blanket over her just as the stable door burst open. Then, like a demented spinning top, the old woman set about the intruders with a broom. The stable lad, seeing the trouble, quickly flung wide the stalls so that the terrified horses were loose, and then he launched himself at Comyn's men with a pitchfork. The boy shouted and cursed, Nan sobbed and screamed, the horses kicked and reared wildly, and in the confusion Agnes slipped silently out of the stable door. The melee behind her, she fled.

Fortunately, Agnes knew the woodland around the hall really well, as she had often hunted there with her father and friends. The day was still sunny and clear so she was able to make good progress through the woods. She was light and made little noise, unlike the fully armed men who were following her. She could hear them crashing through the trees behind her, but was able to hide herself in the shadows and thick brush. At one time she thought she had evaded them, as the sounds of their search began to fade away, but then they must have turned back, realising they had passed her by. After a long time in the woods Agnes saw that the day had turned. As sometimes happens in May, a sudden storm was building up. She seemed to have been in the woods for hours. Her pursuers were obviously not going to give up. What Agnes did not know was that Comyn's words were still ringing in the men's ears: 'Bring her to me and I will reward you well. Come back without her and I will hang every last one of you from the battlements of Whitwick Castle!' They knew that Red Comyn always kept his promises.

Lady Agnes heard the whistles and whoops closing in again. She moved as quietly as she could, but because of the storm it was getting dark in the woods and she was afraid of falling. Suddenly lightning flashed and she saw one of the Scots only a few yards from her, heading in her direction. Fortunately he was looking the wrong way and, just then, she came to an old hollow tree and was able to slip into its darkness. Hardly daring to breathe, she listened as the hunt passed her hiding place and began to fade into the distance.

Agnes stayed hidden for as long as she dared. Soon the hunters would realise their mistake and turn again. They were between her and the road that would lead to her parents and safety. She would have to leave the lands she knew and set out into the fearsome, dark Outwoods and make her way as best she could to the Priory at Grace Dieu. Surely even Red Comyn

would not dare to go after her there. She would ask the prioress for sanctuary.

She struggled her way through the forest, so unlike the friendly woodland near home. She dared not ask for help from any of the peasants who lived and worked here as they would be too afraid of Lord Comyn and would be sure to hand her over. By the time she came out of the forest the rain was falling in sheets. Her clothes had been intended for a May Day celebration not for a headlong race through rough terrain. Across the rugged rocks of Charnwood she staggered, exhaustion dogging her heals. Another flash of lightning showed her the gloomy profile of Beacon Hill and riders outlined against the sky. Thankfully they were heading away from her. Finally the storm passed over and the clouds parted, and the moon emerged to bathe everything in silver light, but Agnes was past noticing. She collapsed on the ground in fear and exhaustion.

The next morning, before the sun came up above the hills, the Hermit of Holywell Haw came out of his hut to pray, as he did every day. However, this day was different. He was barely ten steps from his hut when he saw a strange shape lying in the wet grass. Even in the predawn gloom he could see the golden hair of a young woman. He rushed over to her. Her eyes were closed and she seemed not to breathe. He touched her skin and it was as cold and smooth as alabaster. He knelt by what he feared might be a corpse and prayed as he had never prayed before. Then he gently lifted her and carried her to the holy well. There he used his scallop shell to scoop up the holy water and trickle it between the cold lips, all the time praying to Mary. Miraculously, the blue left the lips and brow and the eyes slowly opened. She was alive!

Word was sent to Groby Hall and Lady Agnes was returned to her loving family. The hermit was thanked and rewarded for his kindness and courage. One year later, Lady Agnes married Edward Grey of Bradgate Park. The young couple were well matched and lived happily together for many years.

Red Comyn continued with his wicked ways for a few more years but, as could be expected, he met a violent death and was mourned by no one. That was not the end of him but, as they say, that's another story!

THE RED WOLF OF CHARNWOOD

About two years after this abortive attempt on Agnes Ferrars, Red Comyn was killed in a fight over a debt that he refused to pay. Far from mourning his passing, the people of Charnwood heaved a collective sigh of relief. Unfortunately, this was not the last of him. Within a few weeks of the fiend's death, a wolf appeared in the area. It was a giant creature with a tangled red pelt. It had a partiality for young flesh, especially tender young girls. It wasn't long before people began to connect the death of the giant Red Comyn with the sudden appearance of this giant wolf whose coat was as long and red as Comyn's hair. Many attempts were made to kill or capture the creature, but all were in vain.

This scourge terrorised the area for many generations right into the next century. Early in 1550, a youth and a girl were riding through Bradgate Park. She was the studious and pious fourteen-year-old Lady Jane Grey and her young friend was Francis Beaumont of Grace Dieu Hall. Jane was a direct descendant of Edward Grey and the Lady Agnes Ferrars, who had escaped the clutches of Red Comyn in the fourteenth century. As they rode round a great rock, an enormous red wolf appeared ahead of them. The terrified horses reared, throwing their riders to the ground before galloping away, leaving the young people defenceless. Francis drew his small dagger and bravely stood between Jane and the wolf. The wolf knocked him down and leapt upon him. As they grappled on the ground, Jane picked up a rock and brought it down on the wolf's head. The creature toppled.

Unfortunately it was only stunned and soon reared up again. Before Francis could do anything the wolf turned on Jane with a savage snarl. Showing amazing courage and cool thinking,

Jane picked up a sharp branch lying nearby. As the great jaws opened, Jane plunged the sharp end into the mouth and down the gaping throat. The wolf gave a bloodcurdling shriek and collapsed dead at the feet of Lady Jane Grey. The young couple started for home and were met on the way by some of her father's men, sent to search for them. The men were amazed at the story of the attack and hurried to collect the body of the wolf. The snarling head of the creature was mounted and displayed in the main hall of Bradgate House.

Sadly there was no happy ending for Francis and Jane. Though Francis Beaumont had shown great courage and loyalty to Jane, he was not considered a suitable match for her. Her father, Henry Grey, Duke of Suffolk, forbade the young people from seeing each other again. Henry Grey had much higher expectations for his eldest daughter.

LADY JANE GREY

Lady Jane Grey lived at Bradgate House in Bradgate Park, Leicestershire, about six miles from the town of Leicester. She was unfortunate to be surrounded by ambitious relatives; her father was Henry Grey, Duke of Suffolk, a man of power and high-standing in Tudor England, and her mother, Frances, was the granddaughter of Mary Tudor, King Henry VIII's younger and favourite sister.

Towards the end of his life, Henry VIII had announced how the crown should be passed on after his death. First in line was his legitimate son, Edward. Should Edward and his two half-sisters, Mary and Elizabeth, all die without issue, the crown should pass to the descendants of Mary Tudor, his beloved

younger sister. When Edward came to the throne as a boy of nine, Lady Jane Grey's position in the Tudor hierarchy made her an exceptionally valuable young woman. She was preceded in rank only by the princesses Mary and Elizabeth.

Unfortunately for Jane, the young King Edward's chief minister, John Dudley, Duke of Northumberland, had a son of marriageable age, Lord Guildford Dudley. Jane's parents saw that a match between Jane and Guildford Dudley would give them great status, and access to wealth and power. In May 1553, Lady Jane Grey and Lord Guildford Dudley were married.

By June 1553 the fifteen-year-old Edward VI lay dying. At his bedside, whispering in his ear, was John Dudley, Duke of Northumberland. Northumberland may have reminded the dying king that his sisters, Mary and Elizabeth, had, at one time, been declared illegitimate by their father, Henry VIII. Though the King had restored them both to the line of succession, he had allowed this illegitimacy to stand. Perhaps Dudley worked on Edward's fear of Catholicism, which the young king had so viciously opposed in his short reign. He may have reminded Edward that Mary, the next in line to the throne, was, like her mother, a convinced and devout Catholic.

Whatever arguments he used, the wily chief minister succeeded. Edward VI declared the Protestant Lady Jane Grey his successor, and on 6 July 1553 he died. The next day Lady Jane Grey was pronounced Queen and took up residence in the Tower of London to await her coronation. The Dukes of Northumberland and Suffolk must have been jubilant with the success of all their plotting. Jane herself, however, was not happy, for she was well aware that she had less claim to the throne of England than Princess Mary.

Unfortunately for Northumberland he had been unable to capture Mary, who had escaped to East Anglia, a Catholic stronghold. There she started to rally her supporters, of which there were many. Mary's mother, Catherine of Aragon, Henry VIII's first wife, had been popular and many felt she had been badly treated by Henry and his ministers. There was a popular uprising and the Privy Council changed sides and declared for Mary. Jane was now a usurper and was imprisoned, along with her husband and their supporters. Jane had been Queen for just nine days.

Northumberland was executed on 22 August 1553. Jane, her husband and other supporters were tried in November 1553 for high treason and were, of course, found guilty. They were all sentenced to death. At first Mary decided to spare Jane's life, but then Sir Thomas Wyatt led a rebellion in protest at the return of Catholicism. Although Jane was in no way connected with this rebellion, her foolish father joined it. The uprising was defeated and Mary was persuaded that Jane could very well prove to be a focus for rebellious Protestants in the future. She should, therefore, be executed.

In 1554 Lady Jane Grey, her husband, and other members of his family, were executed. Most of the executions took place in public, but Jane was beheaded in private, inside the Tower of London, a 'privilege' granted only to royalty. On the scaffold, Jane agreed that her accession was illegal.

Jane's father, the Duke of Suffolk, was executed one week later. Her mother was fully pardoned and allowed to live at court with her two remaining daughters. It is an interesting turn of fate that Elizabeth Bowes-Lyon, the current Queen's late mother, was a descendant of Lady Catherine Grey, Lady Jane Grey's younger sister. I wonder what might have happened if Lady Catherine had been the first daughter and not the second.

Bradgate Park is 850 acres of outstanding history and beauty to the north-west of Leicester. In 1928 the park was bought by Charles Bennion from the descendants of the Greys. Bennion gave the park, in perpetuity, to the people of Leicestershire.

Over time many local legends have grown up around Lady Jane Grey, the Nine Days Queen, and around Bradgate Park. One states that, when Jane was executed, the gardeners at the house chopped off the tops of all the oaks in the park as a mark of respect. Another tells of a ghostly coach that drives through the park on the anniversary of her execution. The coach travels to the now-ruined house or to a local church. Some say the coachman is headless, others that the horses are headless, and still others that the occupant of the coach is headless. All seem to agree that there is a definite shortage of heads!

THE TRAP

Sir Wolstan Dixie of Bosworth Hall was not a happy man. Today was the start of the new season for the Atherstone Hunt, which by tradition always set off from Bosworth Hall.

Because Sir Wolstan's gout was now very bad, he could not ride out with the hounds.

Sir Wolstan was very protective of his youngest daughter, the lady Annabel, for both his other daughters had married and left home. It was she who read to him when he was confined to bed, she who cheered him when he was depressed. He looked up as she rose to leave the breakfast table and saw that she was already dressed for the hunt. He knew his daughter; though she enjoyed the hunt, and the ride out with the hounds, he knew that she would stay towards the back among the tail-end riders, for Annabel hated to see the final kill, the fox cornered by the baying hounds, the blooding. She assured her father she would ride carefully, said she'd give him a full account of the day's hunt at supper that evening. She then kissed him goodbye and left the breakfast room.

As the riders gathered, Annabel noticed that there seemed to be more followers on foot than usual. She saw some familiar faces – the carroty-haired son of the village postman, and his friend who kept ferrets – but there were others whom she had never seen before. The hunt set off, the dogs streaking ahead, and Annabel made sure that she remained at the rear, right at the back, the last of the slower riders.

So when she rode at a particularly difficult fence, and her horse stumbled and threw her, she was alone. Alone and stunned. She lay unable to move until the followers on foot at last caught up and saw what had happened. A young man, a stranger to her, saw that she had damaged her ankle and helped her remount. Then he offered to lead her horse back home.

On the way back to Bosworth Hall she learned a bit about her rescuer; he told her that he worked in the stables at Osbaston, a village a few miles away.

By the time Annabel's ankle had at last healed it was nearly Christmas, and she had to make her yearly round of gift-giving to retired retainers. First she went to all those who lived in the nearby cottages. Next she travelled further afield to visit on old gardener living in the village of Osbaston. That evening she was late home and her father scolded her. 'It's dark. You're late my dear, very late. I was worried about you.'

'No need to worry father, I was quite safe. That lad, the one that brought me home when I sprained my ankle at the hunt, he walked back with me, back from Osbaston. Saw me home.'

Spring was starting to show when Sir Wolstan had a very bad night with his gout. He couldn't sleep so went to his library to try to read. As he sat there he heard a door close, and, looking out of the window, saw a figure in a long hooded cloak cross the courtyard; it went out through the gate into the orchard. Puzzled, he spoke the next morning to the butler, asking who might have gone out so late at night. The butler checked and reported back that none of the staff had admitted to having been outside after dark.

Some nights later, once more unable to sleep, Sir Wolstan was sitting at his library window when he heard the same door close, and saw the cloaked figure cross the courtyard and disappear into the orchard. He thought it was a woman, so the next day he questioned the three female members of his staff. All three swore that they had never left their beds, and never had any wish to be out after dark.

Then, in early April, the gamekeeper came to report to Sir Wolstan that he thought they had a poacher working the estate. In their woods he had found large footprints, with a particularly long stride pattern. The prints were too large, he said, to be anyone local.

'Well then,' said Sir Wolstan, 'tomorrow we go into Leicester. In the big carriage. Have it ready for an early start.'

In Leicester he bought the biggest, strongest mantrap that the blacksmith had in stock. They stowed it on the floor of the carriage, hiding it under some sacking. The next day the trap was laid in the woods, in the exact spot where the footprints had been found.

That evening, after dinner, Sir Wolstan and his gamekeeper
sat in the library, enjoying a drink and a game of chess, and
waited. At midnight they decided to call it a day. The following
evening they watched and waited again. This time the vigil bore
fruit; the figure appeared, crossed the courtyard and vanished
into the orchard.

'Time to go,' said Sir Wolstan, 'I must know who it is that
leaves the house so late in the night.' Carrying lanterns, the two
men went out into the night.

They were in time to see the figure go through the gate to
the orchard. Though it was too dark to see clearly, Sir Wolstan
knew that the only other way out from the orchard was by
the gate into the woodlands. The two followed, keeping their
distance, and had just got into the woodlands when they heard
screams.

'Quick man! Go on, I think we've got him. Hurry, I'll follow.'
And Sir Wolstan limped after his gamekeeper, who was soon
lost to sight. He was a little way further into the woods when
the gamekeeper come hurrying back to him. 'Come no further,
sir, please. 'Tis no poacher that's caught – 'tis a woman sir.'

Sir Wolstan pushed past the gamekeeper, stumbled along the
path, and came to where he could see two figures, clutching each
other. One was caught in the trap that he himself had ordered
to be placed in the woods. The second figure, a stranger to him,
was struggling to force apart the vicious teeth of the trap.

Sir Wolstan staggered, fell against a tree and covered his eyes. Seeing nothing, he yet knew that the blood which pumped onto the path at his feet was the blood of his daughter, the lady Annabel. It seemed to him an age, a lifetime, till she was freed. Then the gamekeeper and the young man lifted her up, while Sir Wolstan turned away, not bearing to see his beloved daughter dead in the arms of the stable boy from Osbaston, killed by his own trap.

THE MISTLETOE BOUGH

The mistletoe hung in the castle hall,
The holly branch shone on the old oak wall

Servants had been working for days to prepare the hall for the great festivities. Henry, Earl of Gainsborough, was well known for the lavishness of his Christmas celebrations. These celebrations he generously shared with all the local gentry in Rutland. No one of importance could afford to miss being at the Earl's castle, lest their standing in society suffer. The festivities were so renowned that, on more than one occasion, the dissenting minister in Stamford had been heard to preach against them. He even denounced the use of evergreens to decorate the hall, claiming that it was evidence of paganism. He prophesied that such extravagance and godlessness would bring down His wrath upon the Earl's head.

When the guests arrived, their carriages and horses were to be met by the many grooms. The stables would be full for most of the twelve nights of Christmas. This year was to be an even more sumptuous affair than usual. The Earl's only child,

Lady Genevra, was to become engaged to the young Lord Lovell. This would be a joining of two powerful families but was also a love match between the two young people, who had been friends and playmates since early childhood. The Earl was especially pleased with the match, because it made his beloved daughter so happy. Genevra had been his pride and joy ever since the all-too-early death of his beautiful and beloved wife Celestra. As the years passed and the child grew to look so much like her mother, the Earl had become a doting and indulgent father who would grant his child whatever she asked. It was a relief to the Earl that his rather headstrong daughter should choose a young man who was so eminently suitable to her standing.

So it was with great pleasure that Earl Henry set in motion the Christmas preparations. All rooms were to be cleaned from the top of the castle to the bottom – even the old attics were to be opened up and tidied, in case any of the multitude of guests needed a secluded place to rest. Fires were lit in all the main rooms and there was a fug of smoke everywhere until all the old birds' nests, trapped in the chimneys, had been burnt. Carpets and rugs were swept and beaten, ornaments and pictures dusted, and the ancient suits of armour polished until they glowed. When all was clean, a vast number of candles were lit and the holly was hung. Lastly, Earl Henry gave the signal to bring in the mistletoe bough.

A team of gardeners struggled into the hall with a massive branch cut from the ancient oak tree which had been felled that morning. Entangled in the branch was a heavy growth of mistletoe. The men hauled up the bough to hang from the rafters. Over their heads the mistletoe hung, with its burden of pale berries, glistening in the light of the candles.

The Great Hall was filled with the sounds of laughter and music. Firelight glinted on fine wine in equally fine crystal glasses. The music was joyful and enticed even the oldest onto the floor to dance. These were the highest-born people from all around. The knights and their ladies dressed in the latest fashion, made from the most costly fabrics to be had. Jewels glinted in hair, and on necks, wrists and fingers. Beautiful perfumes wafted throughout the room. The Earl looked down on his guests from the top of the magnificent main staircase and was delighted to see them having such a good time. Soon he would go down and join in the festivities, but first he had to present his daughter and her betrothed to the assembly.

As the revellers caught sight of Earl Henry at the top of the stairs, a hush fell over the room. Then there was a drawing in of breath and a sigh of collective awe as Lady Genevra appeared beside her father, with Lord Gerard Lovell on her other side. The guests stared in amazement at the vision that was Lady Genevra. She was as tall as her father, though inches short of Lord Lovell. Her face was fairer than the finest alabaster. On her golden hair glowed a coronet of exquisite pearls. Her dress was of white silk, embroidered with small golden flowers, each one with a tiny emerald at its centre. On the hand held by Lord Lovell could be seen an emerald ring, surrounded by more pearls.

At her side, Lord Gerard Lovell was equally impressive. He was a tall and handsome young man. His clothes were of the finest silk, brightly embroidered with the red and blue of his family's coat of arms. His dark red hair shone in the light of the fire and the candles, and all could see the pride and love with which he regarded his betrothed. As the Earl and the young couple descended the stairs, spontaneous and enthusiastic applause broke out all around. On reaching the floor of the hall, Earl Henry called for the musicians to strike up again, and soon the room was filled with music and laughter.

As the night wore on and the young people had almost danced themselves to a standstill, they decided to play a game of hide and seek. The young women would hide and the young men seek. In this way it was hoped to make assignations away from the sharp eyes of the older generation. With a rustle of silks, Genevra led her giggling friends to the upstairs rooms. She helped each to find a suitable hiding place – behind curtains, under beds, inside old cupboards. At last, all were safely secreted about the many rooms and only Genevra was left. So many were hidden that she could think of no more places, and she had no choice but to make her way up to the old attics. There she might find somewhere to hide herself.

Back in the main hall the young men had finished counting and, led by Lord Lovell, were bounding up the stairs to the upper rooms. Amid much laughter and squealing, young women were discovered and hauled from their hiding places, into the light. As each girl was found she joined the search for the rest. Soon there was so much happy shouting coming from upstairs that the older folk decided it was time to take a hand in proceedings. In no time at all everyone was scattered around the upstairs rooms of the castle, and only one person remained unfound. At first everyone thought that Lady Genevra had just been very clever in finding a really good place but, as time wore on and there was no sign of her, the gaiety and the laughter turned to worry.

The Earl and some of his older friends returned downstairs to see if by any chance his daughter had managed to creep past all the searchers. The hall was empty of all but four footmen, each carrying a tray of polished drinking glasses. The fire still burned in the great fireplace, its light reflecting in the crystal goblets. The mistletoe that had grown on the sacred oak, which had been so wantonly felled that day, still swung from the rafters, its pearl-white berries glowing in the flickering light.

Earl Henry spoke hesitantly, ''Tis but a joke to make a trial of our love!' and looked round at his friends, who nodded doubtfully, hoping that he would be proved right. They poured him another glass of wine, which he drank, but those closest noticed that his hand shook. All that night the search continued, then into the next day, but nothing was found. The guests all left, feeling themselves in the way and unable to bear the sad atmosphere in the castle. Young Lovell stayed for a week and then for two, but even he had to leave at last.

From then on there were few visitors to the castle. No one wanted to intrude on the Earl's grief. People were at a loss as to what to say or do for the poor man. For many months the loyal servants kept searching while looking after their distraught master. Though every nook and cranny of the castle seemed to have been searched more than once, no sign of the missing girl was ever found. An air of gloom and sadness descended upon the once-happy household.

The Earl lived on in his castle for many years until he was a very old man, wandering from room to room looking for his lost child. As time passed, more of the castle became neglected and abandoned. And there were fewer and fewer servants to look after such a vast place. As he grew older the Earl's mind became clouded. He knew he had lost something of importance but could not remember what, but he still felt as deeply the pain that the loss caused him. When he finally died, the house passed to a distant relative who had no need of it. It stood empty for a long time.

Many years later the castle was sold with its contents. The new owners decided to sort through all the rooms to see just what they had purchased. They started at the top in the attics, carefully clearing away dust, dirt and cobwebs. In one room was found a fine oak chest. On each side was a carving of a scene from the life of Christ: his birth, crucifixion, entombment and resurrection. There was also a small plaque that told that the chest had been carved by Antony of Trent.

The chest was difficult to open and in the end it was decided to break the lock that held the lid closed. Inside they found not the rich garments they expected but a sad, crumbling skeleton. On the skull, along with a few strands of once-golden hair, lay a lovely coronet set with fine pearls. The dress was but a few wisps of fabric, with a trace of gold embroidery and a few green beads. On the bones of one finger was a ring set with pearls surrounding a glorious glowing emerald.

An old oak chest that had long lain hid
Was found in the castle, they raised the lid
And a skeleton form lay mouldering there
In the bridal wreath of the lady fair.

The lovely Lady Genevra had, at last, been found.

Oh sad was her fate, in sportive jest
She hid from her lord in the old oak chest;
It closed with a spring, and her bridal bloom
Lay withering there in a living tomb.

It is claimed that this story is based on a true event that occurred at Exton Hall in Rutland in the eighteenth century. During a party at the hall, Catherine Noel became trapped in an old chest and died of suffocation. In the 1830s the story was made into a ballad by T.H. Bayly and Sir Henry Bishop. The ballad became one of the most popular ever written and was often sung at Christmas time.

Branwen, Daughter Of Llyr

In the long past and distant time of the ancient Celts, the god Llyr was lord of all the seas and waters around the islands of Britain, and it is told that he fell deeply in love. Now, Llyr's beloved was a woman of the earth, whose home lay at the very centre of the land of Britain, far from the watery realms of her lover. But such was his love for her that Llyr was content to make his seat of power there on earth. And the place where they lived together was called Llyrcester.

In time three children were born to Llyr and his wife, two sons and a daughter. And Bran, the first-born son, became known to the storytellers as Bran the Blessed, for he had both wisdom and courage, and was loved and honoured by the people of Llyrcester for his fair and just dealings. He was, too, a man of great stature, and stood at least three times the height of any other man. It is told that his eyes shone like two deep lakes of water, and the hair of his head rippled in the wind like the leaves on the trees of a dark forest.

The minstrels and storytellers sang too of the beauty of the daughter, Branwen, and told tales of her goodness and gentle nature. These stories spread far and wide, and in time they reached the ears of the King of Ireland. He listened and determined to make Branwen his wife.

Preparations for the long journey across the sea to Llyrcester began. Harpers, minstrels and bards assembled. Baggage carts were loaded with gifts of gold, jewellery, fine cloths and weaving. As many as 100 warriors, mounted on 100 fine horses, rode out with the King and embarked for Britain.

When at last this vast throng arrived at the seat of the god Llyr, there was great rejoicing. The young king from Ireland was welcomed with music with dancing, with feasting, and with stories from the assembled bards. He in turn gave gifts to Llyr and his court. Then he gazed upon Branwen and gave to her his heart. And Branwen looked at the King and saw a man to love, and so the speedily celebrated marriage was a delight to all. To all, that is, except Efnisien, Branwen's younger brother, a dark man full of envy and simmering anger. He had been absent while the marriage was planned and felt himself to have been slighted; none had asked his thoughts concerning the match. Efnisien took himself away from the rejoicing and he raged and sulked and meditated revenge.

Efnisien fumed and fretted and, late in the night, when everyone else was in their beds and sleeping off the effects of the evening's celebrations, he crept into the yard where the hundred horses of the Irishmen were stabled and took his dagger to them. He sliced off the ears, lips and tails of every animal. Straightaway the screams of the mutilated and dying horses woke the grooms. Amid the chaos and confusion, the newly married king awoke. Outraged, insulted, betrayed, he gathered his warriors together and prepared to depart, threatening revenge and long-lasting enmity to Llyr and his followers. Even his new bride he put aside; he spurned her despite her pleadings, her distress.

Then Llyr and Bran took council together, and humbly they appealed to the Irish, swearing that this dreadful deed was done neither at their command nor with their knowledge. And Llyr swore unwavering love for his new son-in-law and gave gifts of silver, swords, and 100 fine fresh horses. In a last attempt to appease the Irishmen, Llyr presented to their king a great cauldron made of bronze. Now, this great cauldron stood the height of a tall man, and it glittered in the sunlight. But above all it had a wondrous and magical power.

'My son, great king, husband to my best-beloved child Branwen, listen well,' said Llyr. 'This mighty cauldron has power to make him who owns it invincible. Any man slain in battle, when he is placed into this cauldron, will be renewed; life will rekindle in the dead warrior so that once more he may do battle for his king.'

And the King, Matholwch, looked at the cauldron and saw that it was deeper than the tallest of his warriors, and he saw that the sides glistened and that, engraved upon the great lid, were the secret symbols of power.

Once more he took Branwen to his heart, and they made ready to return to Ireland. Then Llyr and his wife, and all the people, grieved as they bid farewell to Branwen, but rejoiced in the love that was between her and the Irish king.

In Ireland Branwen was happy with her husband Matholwch, and in time she gave birth to a baby boy. She named him Gwern.

Meanwhile, in Llyrcester, Branwen's mother grew sick and died, and so great was the grief of Llyr that he determined to leave the place where he had lived with his wife and return to his watery realm. He decreed that Bran should rule in his stead.

Then there was, for a while, peace and content in the land. Bran proved himself a just ruler and the people came to love him. This made Efnisien angry and ever more envious of his brother. He decided to go to his sister. He made no farewells but set out at night and took a ship for Ireland. When he reached the court of King Matholwch he was greeted with delight by Branwen, for she had never seen the evil nature of her brother. He was welcomed, too, by the King and his followers and at first all was well, but, in time, seeing how great was the love that the Irish people had for his sister, he grew ever more envious and began to whisper dark lies concerning Branwen. Into the ears of the courtiers he dropped false secrets – that she had strange and evil powers, that she was false to the King, that she took many lovers. Soon people began to believe these stories, and Matholwch himself heard, listened and believed the scurrilous lies told of the woman he had married. Then he too turned against her, put her from him, and ordered that henceforth she was no longer his wife but his servant.

Branwen was put to work in the kitchen, became the scullery maid, and had to clean floors and scrub pots and pans, clean out the fires and sweep the ashes away. She suffered these humiliations with grace and patience, until one day a bird flew into the kitchen and settled at her feet. It was a young starling. She saw that it was hungry and fed it some crumbs, and each day after that it came to her for food. As she held the bird she sang to it and talked, told it her woes, and before long she saw that it seemed to listen to her words, appeared to understand her sorrows. She taught it words and spoke to it of her brother.

'Bran,' she said, 'Bran the Blessed, who is as tall as three men, and his hair blows in the wind like the leaves in a forest of great oak trees. Fly my friend, fly little bird, fly till you come to such a man, fly far and make you a nest in the hairs of his head; fly to him and tell him of his sister.' Then Branwen took paper and wrote of her grief, and when she was done she folded the paper and tied it under the bird's wing, and the bird flew away.

The bird flew far – over the waters of the ocean, over land, over forests and rivers – till it saw a mighty man with hair that streamed in the wind. Wearily the little starling settled on the shoulder of Bran the Blessed, and Bran spied the paper and read of his sister's sufferings.

Then Bran gathered his warriors and set off for Ireland. But while his fighting men boarded their ships, there was no vessel large enough to carry Bran. Therefore he waded through the water, leading his ships. And the breezes of the seas blew and lifted the hair of his head, so that it seemed a mountain approached, and that the branches of the trees upon that mountain shook and swayed with the wind. And those who watched from the shore of Ireland were afraid, for they knew that now there would be a great battle and much slaughter.

Bran led his warriors onto the field of battle, and there were many deaths and many casualties. But at nightfall Bran observed that the armies of the Irish seemed to grow no less, and he remembered the cauldron which Llyr had gifted to King Matholwch.

Now some say that Efnisien, seeing the dreadful slaughter among his brother's men, had a change of heart, a sudden and unwonted honourable impulse, of loyalty to Bran. Yet others claim to know that in the fight he was slightly wounded, and so, becoming exhausted, he lay down to rest. Asleep upon the battlefield, and surrounded by the slain, Efnisien was mistaken for dead and placed with the other corpses into the cauldron, there to await renewal, rebirth. Waking, he tried to lift the great lid, but it was heavy, and in a sudden burst of fury he stretched out his arms and pushed against the bronze sides of the cauldron. Fear and anger gave him added strength, and he pushed so mightily that the cauldron began to buckle. It bulged, cracked, burst into four pieces and, with it, burst Efnisien's heart.

Matholwch heard of the loss of his cauldron and was filled with anger. He turned with renewed fury to battle. And fierce was the fight, and terrible the fighting. Many more were slain, and before nightfall the King himself lay dead on the battlefield. Bran too was mortally wounded, and then, at last, all understood that now there would be victory for neither side. Then all battle ceased.

When Branwen learned that her husband had been killed and her brother wounded, her gentle heart broke from sorrow. Those men left alive did for Bran that which he had desired; they took his head back to the island of Britain and buried it. There it remains to this day, and 'tis said that while the head of Bran the Blessed is turned to look out across the land, the place of the god Llyr, Llyrcester, will remain forever safe and free.

7

LEGENDARY LOCALS

These are the tales of real people whose extraordinary lives and exploits have crossed the threshold between reality and story.

The Guild of Corpus Christi was dissolved under the Chantry Act of 1548, and eventually the corporation bought Corpus Christi Hall for its own use. It cost the town £25 15s 4d. Over the following years the building became the venue for a variety of different happenings: music, feasting, discussions and bear baiting amongst other things. Bear baiting was particularly popular in the sixteenth century, the bear being chained to a post while four or five fierce mastiff dogs were set on it. There was a bear garden very near to the Guildhall, and guests at the civic banquets were often invited to view a baiting between the feast and the dessert. One wonders what that did for the digestion. Accounts show that 4s were paid to two bear-wards for attendance at one of the Mayor's civic banquets.

The authorities also supported the Town Waits – musicians who were employed to perform on the many civic occasions.

They also patrolled the streets of the town at night, and would have been responsible for raising the alarm in the event of fire.

In 1588, the Town Waits were in attendance at the Guildhall to entertain guests during the magnificent feast held by the Mayor and his fellow dignitaries, in celebration of the defeat of the Spanish Armada. At this feast the Mayor entertained Lord Huntingdon and many other notables from the town and the surrounding countryside. Among the guests was Walter Hastings, who had commanded the Leicestershire troops gathered to defend the town and the realm against the Spaniards. Tables were laid down the length of the Great Hall, other guests were seated in the parlour, and, as each main dish was carried to the diners, the musicians played an appropriate song. This victory banquet subsequently became an annual feast and was known as the Venison Feast. One assumes, therefore, that venison was on the menu in 1588.

Two centuries later, in 1805, the Mayor held a 'particularly sumptuous feast' to celebrate another British naval victory: the defeat of the French fleet at the Battle of Trafalgar. On that occasion an 'elegant transparency of the late gallant Admiral Lord Nelson was placed at the upper end of the hall; many excellent and appropriate songs and toasts were given, and the festivity of the day was kept up with great spirit and conviviality until a late hour'.

Over the years the Guildhall has played host to many different events, lectures, meetings and entertainments of various kinds. It has had many uses and many lives, and been the scene of many important happenings in the history of the town. On one occasion, Parliament was convened here. It was the home of Leicester's first police force, and housed, at one time, one of the earliest town libraries in the country.

It has also been a place where people from the town and the surrounding countryside, from all walks of life, could gather. Though the guests at the Mayor's civic entertainments were probably of 'the better sort', poorer, ordinary folk too would have had occasion to visit the hall. Sometimes those occasions would not have been the happiest, for the Guildhall has, over the centuries, also been used as a courtroom and a place of judgement.

At least four times a year the judicial officer, Mr Recorder, came to the Guildhall to preside over the Borough court of Quarter Sessions, at which local people who had committed any criminal offences stood trial. An important visitor, second only to the Mayor in significance, Mr Recorder had a chamber set aside and furnished for him and his servant. The records list that he was provided with:

A trusse beddstead,
a trundle bedde to remeyne in the chambre for the use of
Mr Recorder;
a feyther bedde,
ticke for the bedde;
two bowlsters,
one pillowe,
one woll mattris
and a coverledd for his man's bedde

It was obviously essential that Mr Recorder be made as comfortable as possible, for, young and old, rich and poor, all were liable to fall foul of the law and be brought before him at the Quarter Sessions. It was of the utmost importance therefore that Mr Recorder slept well and was undisturbed. He needed to be refreshed, and have his wits about him, when dealing with the rogues of the town.

One such rogue was eleven-year-old Michael Hansbury, who was sent to the House of Correction for one month in 1848 for stealing three buns. The three buns were valued at one penny. In that same year, William Castings, thirteen, stole 1lb of butter and was sentenced to 'Hard labour for one month at the House of Correction' and to be 'privately whipped in addition'. Thirteen-year-old William Herbert was accused of stealing 'six woolcombes of the value of three shillings and six pence, and six pieces of timber to the value of two shillings'. William Herbert was sentenced to two whole months of hard labour at the House of Correction.

So many others must have stood in the Great Hall awaiting their sentence, and so many stories of folly or fraud have been told within the walls of Leicester's Guildhall. Stories of robbery and deceit, of poaching and drunken assaults, of coiners and counterfeiters, of crimes perpetrated by men such as George Davenport.

GEORGE DAVENPORT

Leicestershire's most famous highwayman, George Davenport, was born in Wigston, just south of Leicester, in 1759. When he was old enough, he was apprenticed to a frame knitter. He did not last there very long though, for, being a lively lad, he did not care to sit at the frame for long hours every day. He wanted a more active life, and, finding himself in some bad company, he soon became something of a tearaway.

George was tall, handsome, and generally liked for his easy-going and generous character. Athletic and high spirited,

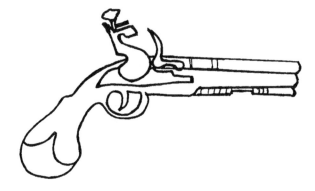

of all the young men in the area he was the most adept – the champion – at wrestling and jumping. He was up to all sorts of escapades, and once danced a jig on the roof of the Crown inn. On another occasion he walked along the top of the battlements of the church, for he loved doing the unexpected and playing jokes, and became a bit of a local hero. A sort of Robin Hood – robbing those he thought rich and giving to the poor people of Wigston and neighbouring Oadby.

Many tales are told of his various exploits, and of his dealings with the recruiting sergeants when they came visiting. These stories gave rise to much laughter among the local folk. When they came recruiting, George would enlist; and then, having pocketed the King's bounty, he would get the sergeant drunk in a session at a nearby inn. This drink would, of course, be at the sergeant's own expense, and as soon as he was asleep and snoring, then George would be off with a pocket full of money and riding the sergeant's own horse. He regularly enlisted and then deserted in this way, waited awhile and then repeated the trick on another regiment. Occasionally he did serve for a while before deserting, and it is known that he did actually serve for some time with the Leicestershire Militia in the

American War of Independence. Rarely was he ever caught after deserting, though we know that he was on one occasion. He was sentenced to 600 lashes for deserting from the 40th Foot Regiment, though they gave up after 300. Mostly he was able to get away scot-free, and in later life confessed to having deserted at least forty times from various regiments.

As a highwayman, he mainly operated on the highways around Leicester, Wigston and Oadby. He was sometimes on horseback, but more often on foot, so he should really have been called a footpad, but a highwayman sounded so much more romantic and flamboyant. He frequently waylaid stagecoaches on the Wigston to Oadby road. His favourite spot was at the point where the coach had to slow down to ford the brook. There was a copse just beside the brook where he used to hide. At the last moment, out popped George to make them 'stand and deliver', and to take any valuables they had with them. The ford is long gone, as the brook now runs in a culvert under the road, but surprisingly the copse still remains in a corner of the grounds belonging to Oadby Town Football Club, just across the road from the Leicester Tigers' practice ground.

Now, as you've probably already guessed, George liked to frequent the inns and alehouses of the neighbourhood, and to enjoy a drink or two. Often he would walk into a pub and proceed to rob the other drinkers of all their cash. Then he would order drinks all round, paying with the money he had just a few minutes before taken off his bemused victims. Often he would end up giving what few pennies were left to the poor. This of course made him very popular with many folks.

One day in the Bull's Head in Belgrave, having bought himself a drink, he noticed a group of men studying a poster: a poster offering a reward for George Davenport!

'I don't think much of that picture,' thought George. 'It makes me look ugly!'

The men were also a bit dubious. 'Does he really look like that?' asked one of them.

'Nah, it's not very good,' said another.

'Oh, you know him then?'

'Well, I've seen him! So I'd recognise him; and I could surely do with that reward money.'

'Couldn't we all,' they chorused. 'But what's going to be the best way to catch him then?'

Soon all sorts of suggestions were being tossed around, while George sat listening, quietly supping his ale, and gleefully planning how to confound them all. Finally he swallowed the last of his drink, put his tankard down, and stood up.

'I'm George Davenport,' he announced. 'So now, catch me if you can!'

With that, he turned and ran out of the door. Well, the men were absolutely gobsmacked, and by the time they had stirred themselves and reached the door, they were just in time to see him leap over a wall and disappear.

On another occasion, he was walking on the footpath from Oadby to Wigston and went some distance with an old man. It was a dark night and so the old man was glad of the company. They made some casual conversation and eventually, warming to George's friendly nature, the man told George how he frequently attended fairs and consequently often returned home late.

'But I make sure my money's safe, for I always hide it in my boots,' he confided.

'Aren't you afraid to travel alone at night?' asked George.

'No, no! There's only one person I'm afraid of.'

'Oh! Who's that then?'

'Why George Davenport, that's who!'

Well it eventually came to the parting of their ways, and George turned to the old man. 'I'm George Davenport,' he said. 'It's time for you to take off your boots and give me the money!' And the poor old man then had no alternative but to do just that.

The beginning of the end came in August 1797, and that end came because George was trying to be a bit too clever. He was caught poaching fish, for which the magistrates fined him £5. As they had not recognised him, he gave his name as George Freer, but was unable to produce the money to pay the fine. So the magistrates ordered that he be kept in gaol. However, on the way from the court to the gaol, they passed the Saracen's Head, and George, being his usual incorrigible self, persuaded his escort to go in for a drink. There, unfortunately, he was recognised by one of the drinkers, and for the sake of the reward was identified as the well-known highwayman George Davenport. So he was back in court, this time on charges of highway robbery and fraud. The jury took only ten minutes to find him guilty, and he was sentenced to be hanged.

Game to the last, George borrowed a chaise and pair from the innkeeper. To the cheers of the crowd, and accompanied by his brother, he drove himself to the gallows on Red Hill at Birstall. On arrival there, and before the noose was placed about his neck, he insisted on wrapping himself in his shroud whilst still wearing all his clothes. He was determined that the hangman should be cheated of his usual perks (these perks being those items of clothing outside the shroud when the body was finally taken down).

George Davenport's wild and colourful career was thus ended. His brother took his corpse back to Wigston, where he was buried in All Saints' churchyard, very close to where he had been born thirty-eight years earlier.

This, and other tales of highwaymen, would have been discussed within the walls of Leicester's ancient Guildhall. There would have been many tales of daring and wickedness, but also stories of remarkable people, of good fortune and mischance, stories of martyrs and heroes, some unsung, others remembered in folk song and tale. Stories of the people of Leicestershire and Rutland.

THE ELEPHANT MAN

Known as the Elephant Man, Joseph Merrick was, in his time, one of the most famous men living in Leicester. He was also the most physically repugnant.

Merrick was a victim of proteus syndrome, an extremely rare condition that caused abnormal growth of the bones, skin and head. The mere sight of his distorted face caused some women to faint, so he donned a mask that covered his misshapen head, a head so large that the cap he wore measured 3ft in circumference. His body was horribly twisted and contorted. His right hand and forearm was a deformed, useless club. Cauliflower-like growths covered his skin. And he emitted a terrible stench that sickened anyone who came near him. A stench that transports us to the regions of the monstrous, the abnormal, the preternatural. A stench that forges a link between the human and the animal, helping to give Merrick his nickname, the 'Elephant Man'. Half-man, half-beast, he was Leicester's very own Minotaur, to be both feared and pitied. To be wondered at, and form the subject of gossip, of stories, and to become the stuff of nightmares, the monster with which to threaten unruly children.

Joseph Carey Merrick was born on 5 August 1862, at No. 50 Lee Street, Leicester, a slum. His mother, Mary Jane, was a teacher. When Joseph was about two years old strange growths started to erupt on his skin, his head grew larger and his right arm became deformed. As he grew older, the condition worsened. When Joseph was ten years old, his mother died of pneumonia. His father remarried and his new bride rejected young Joseph completely.

At twelve years old, Joseph went to work in a cigar factory, but his right arm was now so deformed that he could not fill his quota and he was fired. After trying other jobs, he signed himself into the Leicester Union Workhouse.

Of all the places for Merrick to find himself, an English workhouse was the worst. The lowest ebb of society lived and worked there in exchange for a place to sleep and scarcely enough to eat. But it was whilst he was in the workhouse that Merrick taught himself to read.

Soon he tired of the workhouse, and hearing of Sam Torr, a promoter and music hall showman, Merrick wrote to him asking for work. Torr knew a good thing when he saw it and immediately hired Merrick to appear in his freak show. Joseph Merrick would be an irresistible draw to all those willing to pay good money to view the deformed, the strange, the disfigured.

When surgeon Frederick Treves discovered Merrick in a freak show which had opened in a back room across the street from Whitehall Hospital (now Royal London Hospital), he assumed that the Elephant Man was severely retarded. Treves made arrangements with Merrick's guardian, Tom Norman, to study the man and to present him to a meeting of the London Pathological Society. It was then that Dr Treves made an astounding discovery. Not only was Merrick highly intelligent, but he was literate and a great lover of prose and poetry.

Two years later, Merrick was in Belgium in a freak show operated by a man who cheated him out of his money and then left him stranded in Europe. Somehow Merrick made his way across the Channel and back home to England, but was cornered by a mob of gawkers when he arrived at the Liverpool railway station. Frightened, he gave Treves' card to a policeman and the doctor was called for. Treves hurried to rescue Merrick from the crowds that jostled and jeered at him and took him to Whitehall Hospital.

Now Treves wanted Merrick under his personal care. He knew that he couldn't cure him, but he could make him more comfortable. The hospital board, on the other hand, was adamant that hospital policy forbade permanent patients, especially ones who were public curiosities. They wanted the notorious Elephant Man out of their hospital and into a permanent home, preferably a workhouse.

Hospital administrator Carr Gomm, however, sided with Treves, and he took Merrick's case directly to Queen Victoria. The Queen saw much political value in giving Merrick asylum in a facility that could care for his special needs. She interceded on Joseph's behalf and the hospital board was forced to capitulate.

Merrick was moved downstairs to Bedstead Square, where he was given a small apartment. Treves discovered that, if bathed twice a day, Merrick's odour would vanish. Money was donated to buy Merrick new clothes and, suddenly, he became socially acceptable. The cream of London society came to visit; some out of curiosity and others because it was the trendy thing to do. One of these visitors, a popular actress named Madge Kendal, proved to be a lasting and valued friend.

Even though Merrick was the toast of London, he still craved one thing: the simple ability to lie down and sleep like everyone else. This position was impossible for Merrick. His head was so heavy that if he lay prone, his windpipe would be crushed by the weight and he would suffocate. He slept sitting up, a mass of pillows behind his back and head.

But one night in 1890, Merrick decided that he would experiment. He removed the pillows from his mattress, except one for his head, and lay down. The next morning he was found dead, strangled. He was twenty-eight years old.

Frederick Treves was heartbroken, but not too heartbroken to order Merrick's body boiled down to the skeleton. Then he had the misshapen bones mounted and, along with Merrick's mask, oversized hat, and a model church that Joseph had made, they were displayed in the hospital museum. Merrick's bones are there to this day.

Treves was knighted but the Elephant Man was not forgotten. Ninety years later a film was made by, of all people, comedy producer Mel Brooks. *The Elephant Man* is a loving tribute to an extraordinary man. In essence, the film was a portrayal of a great and courageous human being. If the director took a bit of dramatic licence with the story, he can easily be forgiven, for now the Elephant Man has become the stuff of legend.

THE HORSESHOES AT OAKHAM CASTLE

In appearance, Oakham Castle is unlike most other castles. The present building is all that remains of the Great Hall of a Norman fortified manor house, built by Walkelin de Ferrers in the late twelfth century. It was restored in 1621 and again in 1911.

The court at Oakham Castle is reputed to be the oldest continuously used assize court in England. The court no longer regularly sits at the castle, but, in modern times, a session of the crown court has been held there once every two years. The sitting is preceded by a procession from the nearby All Saints' Church. The Magistrates' Court also used to sit at the castle, but in recent years was transferred to Melton Mowbray.

It is a tradition that peers of the realm visiting the county of Rutland must leave a horseshoe for the castle. More than 200 horseshoes hang on the walls, the earliest given by King Edward IV (1461-1483) and the most recent by the Princess Royal, the Prince of Wales and Princess Alexandra. This unique custom has been enforced for over 500 years, but now it only happens on special occasions such as royal visits, when an outsize ceremonial horseshoe, specially made and decorated, is hung in the Great Hall of the castle.

The upside-down horseshoe appears in the county council's coat of arms and also on the beer bottles of the local brewing company, Ruddles. Although it is thought by some to be bad luck to hang the horseshoe open-end down, here in Rutland it is believed that by hanging the shoe downwards the Devil is unable to sit in the hollow. At the time when the tradition was first enforced, the good people of Rutland needed to keep a strict eye on the whereabouts of the Devil, for he was most certainly hard at work, putting temptation in the way of the people.

JEFFREY HUDSON

Early one morning in 1626, John Hudson and his son Jeffrey left the Shambles in Oakham. They were on their way to Burley-on-the-Hill, the country retreat of George Villiers, Duke of Buckingham, favourite of King Charles I. The father, a 'lusty man', was a butcher by trade, and one of the Duke's bull-wards, responsible for providing bulls and dogs for the popular entertainment of bull baiting.

John Hudson had been summoned to Burley by the Duchess, who wished to inspect Jeffrey. The boy was then nearly eight years old, yet only about 18in in height, and showed no signs of growing any taller. He was, though tiny, perfectly formed, with body, limbs and head all in proportion, and the Duchess had a mind to take him into her household.

As they walked the mile or so up the hill to the great house, one wonders what were the thoughts of the little boy. Used to the harsh conditions of life amongst the lowliest in seventeenth-century England, and to the crowded one-roomed home which he shared with his mother, father, brothers and sisters, he was on his way to meet the highest in the land. He would be leaving his family, all that he had ever known; his life was about to change radically.

Having inspected him, questioned him, and wondered at his diminutive size, the Duchess was charmed by the little creature and it was agreed: Jeffrey would become part of the Duchess's household. However, it was not long before her husband the Duke laid claim to the boy; George Villiers had plans for him. The Duke had been the favourite of both King James I and his son Charles I, but by 1626 his position had begun to grow insecure, and he felt himself threatened by a rival for the King's affections. That rival was Charles' new young bride, Henrietta Maria, daughter of Catherine de Medici of France. Ever since the wedding, the rivalry between the King's favourite and the King's new wife had simmered. It had even fostered a critical hostility between the royal couple themselves. So bad had relations between the King and Queen become, that the French court had been drawn into attempting to end the marital conflict.

George Villiers knew himself to be envied and distrusted, both by the rest of the court and by the populace at large. He therefore needed all the friends he could muster. Even his rival, young Henrietta Maria, might prove a useful ally, if only he could find some way to please her and lessen her unhappiness. Perhaps then the strains between the royal couple would diminish, and his own position become more comfortable.

The Queen was still very young – a mere girl at seventeen years old – and was both vulnerable and lonely, for most of the 400-strong entourage which had accompanied her to England had been sent back to France. She was a Catholic girl married to a Protestant king, living in a Protestant country. Young, alone, angry and very unhappy, she turned to the animals (with which she had surrounded herself) for love and affection. Jeffrey Hudson – the 'fairy' boy, the perfect miniature man – would be just the pet, the toy, to bring some joy and love into the Queen's life. He would also be the lynchpin in Villiers' plan to re-establish himself as favourite to the King.

The journey from Oakham to London took several days. Travelling in the carriage with the servants, the baggage and equipment of the household, Jeffrey could see little from the windows. Above the rattle and shake of the heavily loaded carriage, he could hear the sounds of the great city: shouts, curses, dogs barking, the clatter of hooves on cobblestones; and he could smell the smoke from hundreds of chimneys, the smells of a crowded city with its many churches, markets, theatres, latrines and bear pits.

At York House, the Duke's London home, Jeffrey stepped into a whole new world, a world of painted ceilings, magnificent carvings and furniture, lavish hangings and tapestries, and a collection of the finest paintings. George Villiers was not only an avid collector, but also a showman, a master of display and ceremony, and a superb host. He had planned a feast for the royal couple that would culminate in a presentation to the young queen.

Coached in the part he must play, Jeffrey was first fitted with a sky-blue masking suit, complete with miniature helmet and breastplate. Then he waited, hidden under the great piecrust provided by the cooks, to be carried into the banqueting hall. The musicians played and then fell silent, the trumpets sounded, the chatter of voices stilled, and the great pie was borne into the hall and presented to the Queen. She was handed a ceremonial knife and was about to pierce the pie when the crust began to lift by itself, revealing a tiny hand. Next a small face peered out, two eyes looked into hers, and Jeffrey stepped forth from the pie and bowed. A tiny 18in child – a perfect pet for a lonely queen.

Now Jeffrey was the Queen's dwarf, much loved, petted and mothered by her. He, in turn, was devotedly loyal to her. He learned to read and write and became a Catholic. For about twenty years he was an important member of her household. Though viewed as a pet, a plaything, a butt of laughter for the other courtiers, he yet managed to become a fearless horseman and an expert shot. He was with Queen Henrietta Maria through all the dangers she encountered during the Civil War. He travelled with her, escaped with her to France when the Parliamentary forces began to prevail against the Royalist cause, and was with the Queen when news came of her husband's capture by the Roundheads.

From the age of eight, Jeffrey was constantly at the Queen's side. It was only to save his life that, after twenty years of faithful attendance, she was forced to send him away. During the Queen's enforced stay in France, and at nearly thirty years of age, Jeffrey began to feel that he could no longer endure the indignity of being regarded solely as a plaything, a freak, a clown. Though miniature, he was a man, and should be accorded the dignity of a man. He let it be known that he was prepared to challenge to a duel anyone who mocked him for his size. The court thought this a fine jest and the young bloods continued to bait 'little Jeffrey' mercilessly.

It was time to make a stand and so he issued a challenge. It was accepted by a man named Crofts. And, though duelling was punishable in France by imprisonment and fines, the two met. Both fired but Jeffrey was the better shot; his bullet pierced young Crofts' temple, killing him outright. The Queen was horrified. Jeffrey was forced to depart for his own safety.

This one moment cost Jeffrey his position with the Queen, and proved the second turning point in his life. Young Crofts lay dead in the little French town of Nevers, and Jeffrey's life took another bizarre twist. He rode away from all he had known since the age of eight and headed back to England. At the coast of France, he boarded a ship and sailed for the country he had not seen for some time. But he was not destined to reach home yet; the ship he sailed in was taken by Barbary corsairs. As he later told it, it was a Turkish pirate who took him and carried him to Barbary, where he was sold and remained a slave for many years.

We know little about this time of his life, but it seems that, though totally unsuited to the very hardest physical labours that some slaves were put to, he must have been forced to do much hard work. Slaves captured by the Barbary corsairs were frequently taken in order to be exchanged for ransom. But these captives had to arrange their own ransom. Jeffrey's family were far too poor to pay anything for his release, and it seems that the Queen Henrietta Maria knew nothing of his predicament. Besides, she had other griefs to deal with; in 1649 King Charles I was beheaded by the government of the Commonwealth.

It was not until the Restoration of the monarchy, and the return of Charles II to England, that money was raised by the government and many slaves were ransomed. At last, after nearly twenty-five years as a slave, Jeffrey finally returned to Oakham, to the one brother still alive. Curiously, it is noted that during his time in slavery Jeffrey began to grow. He returned a short man of 3ft 9in. He was no longer the impossibly small miniature man beloved by the Queen; no longer the fantasy figure stepping out of an enormous pie. Just a very short man.

Jeffrey suffered one further imprisonment when anti-Catholic fears were ignited by the malicious lies of Titus Oates (another Oakham man). He spent two years in the Gatehouse prison. Jeffrey died some time in 1681 and has no known burial place. His only memorial is three portraits, painted during the early years when he was Lord Minimus, the Queen's dwarf. A sad end to an extraordinary life which had been full of change, danger and difficulties. A life also of glamour and excitement, and the friendship of a queen.

DANIEL LAMBERT

Daniel Lambert was Leicester's fattest man; his image appears on mugs and plates, pencil cases, boxes of tissues and tea towels. And just consider that, at the time, most people in this country would have been considerably thinner than we are today. As Daniel grew more and more enormous, he must have seemed like a character from the world of fairy tale. One might imagine that he had incurred the wrath of some wicked fairy and been placed under a spell to grow and grow and grow.

Daniel Lambert also earned himself a reputation as a benevolent jailer, who was always interested in his prisoners' welfare. At the comparatively young age of twenty-one, in 1791, he had succeeded his father as keeper of Leicester Gaol, in which position he introduced improvements which earned him the good will of those behind bars, and the respect of many prison reformers of the time. John Howard, an active prison reformer, visited the gaol, and noted the improvements that had been made since a previous visit. Prisoners were no longer hampered by the chains which they had been forced to wear, even whilst taking exercise. And the courtyard in which they exercised had been enlarged. The gaol was whitewashed once a year and kept remarkably neat and clean.

Although born and raised in Leicester, Daniel had moved to Birmingham, serving four years as an apprentice at an engraving and die-casting works. At this time there was no sign of excess weight; in fact, he was a keen sportsman and extremely strong. He was an expert in sporting animals, and was widely respected for his expertise with dogs, horses and fighting cocks. On his return to Leicester, as well as his duties as keeper of Leicester Gaol, he continued his sporting activities.

It is recorded that, on one occasion, he fought a bear in the streets of Leicester. Whilst he was watching a dancing bear on display in Blue Boar Lane, his dog slipped loose and bit the creature. Unsurprisingly, the bear turned on the dog and knocked it to the ground. Lambert shouted at its keeper to restrain his bear so that he could retrieve the dog. Instead of restraining the animal, however, the keeper removed the bear's muzzle, so that she was free to attack the dog. In desperation, Lambert struck the bear with a pole and, with his left hand, punched its head, knocking it to the ground. The dog escaped.

Although Daniel Lambert did not eat large amounts of food, at about the time of his return to Leicester his weight began steadily to increase, and, by 1793, he weighed 32 stone. Concerned for his fitness, in his spare time he devoted himself to exercise, building his strength to the point where he was easily able to carry five hundredweight. Despite his increasingly large girth, Lambert remained fit and active.

By 1801, Lambert's weight had increased to about 40 stone. Although he retained his reputation as a good gaoler, serious concerns were being raised about his fitness for the job. His type of gaol was being replaced with forced labour institutions, and, in 1805, Lambert's gaol was closed, leaving him without employment. However, Leicester magistrates granted him an annuity of £50 a year in recognition of his excellent service as gaoler.

Lambert moved just a few miles across the county boundary to Stamford in Lincolnshire, and in March 1806 the *Stamford Mercury* reported that he was having a carriage specially built 'to convey himself to London'. On his arrival in London in April, he rented an apartment at No. 53 Piccadilly. He then weighed 50 stone. With no employment, Daniel now meant 'To exhibit himself as a natural curiosity', or so the posters advertising him read.

EXHIBITION

****

Mr LAMBERT of LEICESTER

The heaviest man that ever lived

Weighing upwards of 50 STONE

14 POUND to the STONE

**Mr LAMBERT will see company
at his apartments
No.4, Leicester Square**

From 11 O'CLOCK TILL FIVE

Admission ONE SHILLING each

It was at this time that he sat for the artist Ben Marshall, who painted the famous picture of Daniel which accompanies most accounts of his life.

Daniel did not enjoy exhibiting himself as a curiosity, and some six months later he returned to Leicester, where he lived privately. However, in December 1806 he went on tour again. The standard admission fee to see Daniel Lambert was 1s, a considerable sum for that time. No doubt this high entrance fee was intended to keep the masses away.

In 1809, after further tours, Daniel Lambert arrived in Stamford for the races. He took a room at the Waggon & Horses but died suddenly on the evening of 21 June. It was necessary to remove part of the wall of the ground-floor room to remove his body. His enormous coffin was fitted with wheels, and it took twenty men to lower it into his grave in St Martin's churchyard. His tombstone reads:

> In Remembrance of that prodigy in nature Daniel Lambert a native of Leicester who was possessed of an exalted and convivial mind and, in personal greatness had no competitor: He measured three feet one inch round the leg and weighed fifty two stone eleven pounds. He departed this life on the 21st of June 1809 aged thirty nine years. As a testimony of respect this stone is erected by his Friends in Leicester.

Many of Daniel Lambert's possessions are exhibited in Leicester's Newarke Houses Museum, including a selection of his made-to-measure clothes and his large chair; seeing how many children can fit on the giant-sized piece of furniture causes great glee amongst visiting school parties. But it is learning the story of this gigantic man that leaves them open-mouthed and spellbound.

LAURENCE SHIRLEY, EARL FERRERS

Through the packed masses lining the roadsides, the landau made its slow progress. In the coach, the Earl and his companion had plenty of opportunities to examine the unwashed citizens of London. People were packed in at least six deep on the edges of every road. Laurence Shirley, 4th Earl Ferrers, gazed in irritation and contempt at the mob, these dregs of humanity, for they were hampering his progress to an important appointment.

There would be no opportunity for the Earl to change his mind regarding the destination of his journey. Preceding the Earl's landau was a considerable body of Horse Grenadiers and a carriage containing Mr Sheriff Errington and his undersheriff, Mr Jackson. Behind the Earl's landau were two other carriages, one containing friends of the Earl. Finally, at the back of the procession, came another body of military. Not that Earl Ferrers would contemplate making any change to this, the culmination of his story, nor to the life that had led up to it.

The morning of 5 May 1760 had dawned bright and clear; it was a day of promise, when great things should be accomplished. Laurence Shirley had slept surprisingly well and had woken with a clear head (something that had been unusual throughout most of his adult life). He had chosen his clothes carefully – a white silk suit embroidered with silver. It was the suit he had been married in. At 9 a.m. the procession started. It would take two and three quarter hours to reach its destination – the scaffold at Tyburn.

Born on 18 August 1720, Laurence Shirley had royal Plantagenet blood in his veins and was a descendant of the Earl of Essex, Elizabeth I's favourite. In 1745, at the age of twenty-five, Laurence Shirley became 4th Earl Ferrers. Such ancient lineage might be expected to lead to nobility of character. In Laurence Shirley's case this did not happen. With his title he inherited estates in Leicestershire, Derbyshire and Northamptonshire, and made his home at Staunton Harold in north-west Leicestershire.

The Earl had gained an early reputation for having a frighteningly violent temper when drunk. And he was intoxicated most of the time. His anger was often turned against his servants. On one occasion, a young servant refused to verify a false claim that the Earl had received some bad oysters from London. Earl Ferrers flew into a rage, beat the man with a candlestick, and then stabbed and kicked him. Another time, despite having laid some successful wagers at the racecourse at Derby and having pocketed £50 in winnings, the Earl took it into his head that one of his young grooms had been passing information and tips to his rival punters. He became so enraged at this thought that he set about any servant that came within sight with a horsewhip, screaming abuse at them and hurling anything that came to hand.

It was not only his servants who had cause to be wary of arousing his anger; his fellow peers also had reason to fear his violent temper. Few of them would accept an invitation to Staunton Harold, for even at his sunniest the Earl was unpredictable. Nor were his own family spared. One visit by Lord Ferrers' younger brother and wife ended when a minor dispute between the brothers led to the Earl threatening to kill his visitors. They were only saved by a brave servant warning them that the Earl was busy loading a brace of pistols. They left Staunton Harold hurriedly, at 2 a.m.

Lord Ferrers' appetite for strong drink was matched by his appetite for women, the younger the better. In 1743 Margaret Clifford, the young daughter of Ferrers' land agent, caught his eye. Between 1744 and 1749 she bore him four daughters. Despite this liaison, in 1752 he married Mary, the sixteen-year-old youngest daughter of Sir William Meredith. The Meredith family came from Cheshire and perhaps, at that distance, were unaware of his reputation. This match was important to Lord Ferrers as he needed the young woman to provide him with a legitimate heir to his title and fortune. It must also have seemed a good match for the Meredith family; at least, that is, at the beginning of the marriage. However, it was not long before the young woman came to fear for her life.

After suffering her husband's unpredictable moods and unwarranted cruelty for some time, Mary escaped back to her father's household. While under her father's protection, she applied to Parliament for redress. Parliament, most unusually for the eighteenth century, granted her a separation. Maintenance for her was to be raised from her husband's estate. They then appointed trustees for her, and the trustees asked John Johnson, Earl Ferrers' own steward, to oversee the arrangements. At first this worthy man was reluctant to take on such a role, because he felt that it would bring him into conflict with the Earl. Oddly enough, it was Laurence Shirley himself who finally persuaded Johnson to take on the duty. At this time, he regarded Johnson with favour, considering him to be honest and trustworthy.

Mr Johnson lived at Lount, about half a mile from Staunton Harold. In time, however, Ferrers came to dislike Johnson, for he began to believe that the steward had conspired with his enemies to cheat him out of property that the Earl thought was his by right. He demanded that Johnson vacate the farmhouse at Lount. However, under the Act of Separation, the trustees had granted the steward the lease, so he was able to remain in his house. This the Earl added to his list of grievances against John Johnson.

One Sunday in January, Earl Ferrers sent a message to Lount, ordering the steward to come to Staunton on the following Friday, 18 January, at 3 p.m. precisely. His Lordship dined at 2 p.m. that Friday. Having sent all his male servants away on various errands, he then arranged for his mistress, the neglected Margaret Clifford, to take their daughters out for the afternoon and not return until 5.30 p.m. Now there were only three women servants in attendance at Staunton Harold. John Johnson arrived at 3 p.m. as had been arranged and was admitted to the hall. He was taken into the Earl's own room, where His Lordship promptly locked the door. Ferrers then proceeded to charge the steward with various villainies and ordered the frightened man to kneel and beg forgiveness. Johnson went down on one knee but this was not good enough for the enraged peer.

Listening outside the door, the terrified maidservants heard, 'Down on your other knee! Declare that you have acted against me. Your time has come – you must die.' And then a shot. Next they heard the poor steward begging. Begging to be spared. There was a moment of silence, then the Earl unlocked the door and swept out, leaving the three maidservants to rush to John Johnson's aid. One dashed out to summon the nearest surgeon, Mr Kirkland, from Ashby-de-la-Zouch, while a second hurried to fetch Mr Johnson's daughter. Daughter and doctor arrived within a short time of each other.

Lord Ferrers followed Miss Johnson into the room where her father lay. He needed to persuade her not to prosecute. To that end he made promises, swearing that he would look after her and the other members of the Johnson family if she agreed not to start any prosecution against him. And he did his utmost to convince her that her father was more frightened than hurt – despite the evidence of her own eyes.

His Lordship then left the doctor with the injured man, and set about the serious business of drinking himself into oblivion. The more he drank the more irascible and unpredictable he became. He had, however, enough sense to realise the danger he had put himself in, and made an effort to persuade Mr Kirkland, the surgeon, that it was not in his best interests to testify against someone of his standing in society. At one point he went back to see the wounded man, and in pure malice pulled off his wig and threatened to shoot him through the head. He refused to allow the steward to be removed to his own home at Lount, swearing, 'He shall not be removed; I will keep him here, to plague the villain.'

Finally the Earl was overcome by the quantity of alcohol he had drunk and fell into bed, sometime between 11 and 12 p.m. Mr Kirkland immediately arranged for the dying man and his daughter to be taken to the relative safety of their own home in Lount. There Mr Johnson died at about 9 a.m. the next morning.

The news of the murder spread rapidly and neighbours began to gather at Staunton Harold. Many, expecting trouble, had armed themselves suitably, to apprehend the murderer of the well-respected John Johnson. For the next four hours little was seen of Earl Ferrers. He did, however, refuse to be taken into custody and called them all liars when they told him that Johnson had died of his wound. A local collier, named Curtis, then spotted His Lordship walking on the bowling green at the back of the hall, carrying a blunderbuss, two pistols and a dagger. Curtis was a brave (or foolhardy) man and walked up to the peer, and for some reason Ferrers surrendered to him.

The inquest declared that Johnson had been murdered, but because of Ferrers' rank, a local court could not try him. He was sent to London to be tried by his peers in the House of Lords. The Earl was held in the Tower of London. During his incarceration, his alcohol intake was greatly reduced. He was only allowed two pints of wine and a little brandy each day!

It may have been this comparative temperance that led to his downfall. When it came to his trial, Earl Ferrers had to represent himself. This he did extremely well, putting forward his case lucidly and consistently. Unfortunately, as his main defence was that he was a lunatic, his sobriety and calm demeanour did him no favours. Despite the testimony of many witnesses to his 'madness' and 'lunatic outbursts', his peers found him sane and sentenced him to hang at Tyburn and his body to be anatomised.

As they drew slowly nearer to Tyburn, the Earl had no regrets about the way he had spent his life. However, he did feel that his fate was rather unjust; after all, a man of his standing should not be castigated for the treatment of his wife. And as for Johnson, well, he was a rogue and had been disloyal to the hand that fed him.

One thing troubled him; Earl Ferrers was very disappointed that the King had refused his request to be beheaded like the gentleman he was. As a member of the nobility, an aristocrat, he surely had the right to a good beheading, just as his ancestor the Earl of Essex had enjoyed. But as he mounted the scaffold he put these thoughts aside. All would soon be over and he

had ensured that he would make a good end. He was pleased
with himself; he had bribed the hangman to make sure he
would die quickly by pulling on his legs. In that way his neck
would snap and he would not suffer the agonising slow death
of strangulation. Money and station in society could always
ensure things went your way in the end.

Unfortunately for Earl Ferrers, he could never tell one
member of the lower classes from another, and he had given the
bribe to the wrong person. At the relevant time the hangman
and his assistant were too busy fighting over the purse to
pay any attention to His Lordship's suffering. Poor Laurence
Shirley. Too late in the day he learned that you cannot ever rely
on the lower classes to carry out their duties properly.

An Ordinary Woman

He was about to ask her for a light. She knew – she was quite
certain – that any moment now he would turn to her, lower
his head, look her full in the face and ask her for a light. She
had been conscious of him pressed up against her, had felt him
fumble for the cigarette packet and slowly, almost dreamily,
pull one out and place it between his lips. Then he had patted
his pockets for the matches.

It was no use saying that she didn't smoke – pointless, even
dangerous – to pretend that she didn't. No. He'd been in the
waiting room with all the others, with the soldiers shouldering
their bulky kit bags, the women laden with misshapen
shopping bundles. Standing slightly apart from the press of
other travellers, waiting, waiting and watching, he had seen her
light up.

She clutched at the bag on her lap, could feel her hands clammy and knew that she must turn to look him in the face. Be bold, be friendly, but not inviting. He smiled, showing large clean teeth, an arrogant Nazi officer smile, 'Fräulein ...,' he waved his unlit cigarette in front of her.

Yes, she had matches – two boxes in the right-hand pocket of her jacket, impossible to tell them apart by touch alone. In one, a few precious unused matches and some burnt ones. In the other box, a few matches, some used, some unused, and a scrap of paper containing the coded message. But in which box had she hidden the message? Calm, keep calm; give him whichever box comes first to hand. Trust that he'll give the box back when he's finished with it.

She saw him strike the match and light up, heard a contented sigh as he took a first long draw on his cigarette and watched him pocket the box. Then he turned away from her, to gaze out at the countryside. They were nearly there; she could see the terracotta roofs of the little town. Would he get off here, at Roquebrune, at her stop? Could she stay on, travel further, and avoid him as they passed through the exit? No, dangerous to even think of doing that. And the others, the rest of the circuit, they must be warned, told about the lost message. By now Eliane was certain that the matchbox that lay in the officer's pocket was the one that harboured the fatal scrap of folded code. Anytime soon he would want another smoke; out in the street or back in his barracks he would pull out the box, find the message, and she and all the circuit would be discovered. She must get to the safe-house and warn them.

As she hurried through the streets, she felt in her pocket and fingered the remaining box. Once in the safe house, she pulled it out, opened it and saw the matches. Nothing else in the matchbox. Trembling now, she tried to shut it, fumbled and dropped the box. Matches spilled onto the floor and the box split open. There lay the screw of paper. This time the message had got through safely.

Eliane Sophie Browne-Bartroli, born in 1917 to a French mother and English father, was multilingual and lived in Leicester until the outbreak of hostilities. Her husband, Tom Plewman, was an officer in the royal artillery. In the January of 1943, these facts alerted the SOE to possibilities; a highly intelligent young woman, speaking perfect French, married to an officer serving with the British army, no children … this young woman seemed to be the ideal Special Operations Executive, and, following an interview conducted entirely in French, the SOE recruiting officer wrote on her file 'her background makes her entirely suitable for top secret work'.

The SOE was established after Dunkirk to courier secret messages, liaise with the various resistance groups in occupied France, organise and carry out acts of sabotage, and 'set Europe ablaze'. So, in the early months of 1943, Eliane began her training; she learnt to handle firearms, grenades, explosives and had instruction in the various modes of sabotage. There was parachute training, and she would have had to acquire the skill, essential for any undercover operator, of blending in with the local civilian population.

Having completed her training, in August 1943 Eliane was dropped from a 161 Squadron bomber to tumble through the night sky into German-occupied France. As her parachute opened, she drifted down to land near a small farm. She could hear the farmer's guard dogs barking as she hit the ground. She undid the parachute, folded it small, and hid it in some bushes, then realised that her ankle pained her – she had sprained it in the landing. But more importantly, and much more alarming, there was no sign of her contact, the person who should have been there to meet her, to set her on her way. The first vital link with her network, her 'circuit', was broken.

Eliane knew not to linger, so she began her journey alone and unsure. Eventually she was able to make contact with the circuit, codenamed Monk, and then she learned that the man who should have been at the place of her drop had been captured by the Germans that evening.

So began her clandestine life as Madame Prunier, housewife of the town of Marseille. Going about her daily life, travelling by train or by road, she carried messages to and from the radio operator based in Roquebrune. Madame Prunier also transported the dynamite and the fuses needed for sabotage operations. In March 1944 alone the circuit carried out nearly thirty-two acts of sabotage, and derailed two trains, closing the line between Toulon and Marseille for four days.

As she went about her secret and perilous life, meeting parachute drops, and acting as guide and support to newly arrived agents, Eliane must, at times, have thought back to her life in Oadby, to her husband, away serving in the British army, fighting, just as she was, the Nazi menace. A beautiful woman, young and highly intelligent, it is difficult to believe that she did not attract the interest of the men she met on her travels. However, it was another woman who proved to be the spark which brought about the betrayal she always knew possible. That woman, known as Alberte, was seeing two different men, and, unknown to her, one of the two, Bousquet, was a secret Gestapo agent. It did not take him long to learn about the other man, to uncover many of the secrets of the circuit, and discover the address of the flat in Marseille where Madame Prunier lived.

A few days later, when the leader of the circuit arrived at the flat, he was captured by Gestapo agents posing as gasmen. Then they cleared away all signs of the struggle and waited for Madame Prunier to walk, unsuspecting, into the flat.

On 13 September 1944, in the notorious concentration camp at Dachau, Eliane Plewman, along with some of her comrades from the Monk circuit, faced a Nazi firing squad. After the war she was posthumously awarded the Croix de Guerre with Bronze Star, and the King's Commendation for Bravery. On the Dachau memorial to British officers her name appears, one of the thirty-nine SOE women agents who were sent to France during the war. Thirteen of these women never returned.

BIBLIOGRAPHY

BOOKS

Anon, 'King Leir and his Three Daughters', *A Book of Old English Ballads* (1896)

Banner, John W., *Discovering Leicester* (1991)

Barber, Richard (ed.), *Myths and Legends of the British Isles* (1998)

Beare, Beryl, *England: Myths & Legends* (1996)

Bell, David, *Leicestershire & Rutland: Tales of Mystery & Murder* (2002)

Bennett, J.D., *Leicestershire Portraits* (1988)

Binney, Marcus, *The Women who Lived for Danger* (2003)

Bott, D.J., 'The Murder of St Wistan' (1953 pamphlet)

Briggs, Katharine, *A Dictionary of British Folk Tales* (1971)

Chambers, *Book of Days* (1864)

Dunkling, Leslie and Wright, Gordon, *The Wordsworth Dictionary of Pub Names* (1994)

Geoffrey of Monmouth, *Historia Regum Britanniae* (*c.* 1190)

Greater Wigston Historical Society, 'History of Greater Wigston' (1967 pamphlet)

Green, Susan E., *Selected Legends of Leicestershire* (1971)

———, *Further Legends of Leicestershire and Rutland* (1971)

Meadows, Jack, *Leicestershire: Some Legends and Stories* (1990)

Nicholas, Elizabeth, *Death be not Proud* (1958)

Page, Nick, *Lord Minimus* (2002)

Palmer, Roy, *Folklore of Leicestershire and Rutland* (1985)

———, *English Country Songbook* (1986)

Pegden, N.A., *Leicester Guildhall* (1981)

Readers Digest Association (eds), *Folklore, Myths and Legends of Britain* (1973)

Slater, Alistair R., *Ghostly Tales and Hauntings of South Leicestershire* (1992)

Swift, Eric, *Folk Tales of the East Midlands* (1954)

Tongue, Ruth L., *Forgotten Folk Tales of the English Counties* (1970)

NEWSPAPERS

Leicester Mercury archives

WEBSITES

Wistow.com

Stand-and-deliver.org.uk

The Newgate Calendar

Scarystories.ca

Historylearningsite.co.uk

Diningpubs.co.uk (Ram Jam Inn)

Songs

'Oakham Poachers', *A Short History of John Kirkpatrick*, Topic Records Ltd (1994)

Bold Nevison: Seventeenth-century ballad sung by Joseph Taylor, recorded by Percy Grainger in 1908

Illustrations

Illustration of the Witches of Belvoir from a pamphlet first published in 1619

Illustrations on pp. 97, 131, 139 © Jennifer Briancourt

If you enjoyed this book, you may also be interested in…

Staffordshire Folk Tales

THE JOURNEY MAN

Staffordshire has a long history of ordinary folk encountering magical things. Many travellers have passed through its lands, dropping the odd tale into the mix. Despite the Industrial Revolution and the laying down of motorways, the stories have remained and have often developed in response to changing times. They have always been under the surface, ready to be shared with any who would stop for a while and look a little closer.

978 0 7524 6564 7

Nottinghamshire Folk Tales

PETE CASTLE

Ranging from the silly to the gory and unsettling, *Nottinghamshire Folk Tales* features tales of love, murder, and all kinds of roguery. This book presents the history of the people of Nottinghamshire through the stories they have told and passed on, keeping alive the rich history of events, ideas and customs. Whether the stories are of national import or local folklore, Pete Castle has made them accessible and enjoyable.

978 0 7524 6377 3